JUMBLE®

BrainBusters

5

Dare to Jumble!

David L. Hoyt and Russell L. Hoyt

TRIUMPH
BOOKS

CHICAGO

This book is available in quantity at special discounts
for your group or organization.

For further information, contact:

Triumph Books
601 South LaSalle Street
Suite 500
Chicago, Illinois 60605
(312) 939-3330
FAX (312) 663-3557

Printed in the United States of America

ISBN 1-57243-548-8

CONTENTS

Beginner Puzzles

Intermediate Puzzles

Advanced Puzzles

Answers

JUMBLE®

BrainBusters

BEGINNER
PUZZLES

STARTS WITH AND ENDS WITH A VOWEL

Unscramble the Jumbles, one letter to each square, to spell words that start with and end with a vowel.

#1 LAIEG

#2 REAOP

#3 GIAEM

#4 GAIANU

#5 KEERAU

#6 MICENO

#7 CAVENDA

Arrange the circled letters to solve the mystery answer.

Box of Clues

Stumped? Maybe you can find a clue below.

- Musical drama
- Picture
- Type of lizard
- _____ tax
- Mean, norm
- Used to express triumph on a discovery
- Marked by ready ability to move with quick, easy grace
- Move forward

MYSTERY ANSWER

ANIMALS

JUMBLE. BrainBusters

Unscramble the Jumbles, one letter to each square, to spell names of animals.

#1 CUKD

#2 EGIRT

#3 RONIH

#4 KNUKS

#5 NAPAD

#6 ETRTUL

Interesting Animal Facts

It takes the deep-sea clam about 100 years to grow to a length of one-third of an inch.

A baby giraffe is about six feet tall at birth.

Arrange the circled letters to solve the mystery answer.

MYSTERY ANSWER

JUMBLE JOKES

JUMBLE BrainBusters

Unscramble the mixed up letters to reveal the punch lines as suggested by the jokes.

#1 What canine keeps the best time?

HGACDOWAT

#2 What do you get if you cross a snowman with a vampire?

TFTBEOIRS

#3 What do prisoners use to call each other?

NECLHOESPL

#4 What can you serve but not eat?

LAOVLBLLYEA

#5 What animal never needs a haircut?

GBLEAALAED

#6 What do you call a snowman in the summer?

DPAULED

#7 What do you get when you cross a cheetah and a hamburger?

TAOSFODF

SPORTS

JUMBLE BrainBusters

Unscramble the Jumbles, one letter to each square, to spell words related to sports.

#1
CKPU

#2
ACHCO

#3
NETISN

#4
CSEORC

#5
EEFRERE

#6
FUIOMRN

Interesting Sports Facts

A baseball hit by a bat can travel as fast as 120 miles per hour.

A total of 602 athletes from the United States competed at the Olympics in Sydney, Australia, in 2000.

A croquet ball weighs one pound.

Arrange the circled letters to solve the mystery answer.

MYSTERY ANSWER

MAKING MOVIES

Unscramble the Jumbles, one letter to each square, to spell words related to making movies.

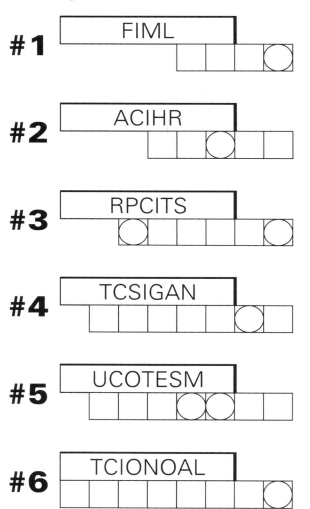

#1 FIML

#2 ACIHR

#3 RPCITS

#4 TCSIGAN

#5 UCOTESM

#6 TCIONOAL

Box of Clues

Stumped? Maybe you can find a clue below.

- Written directions
- The assignment of parts and duties to actors or performers
- Director's _____
- Radiation-sensitive tape
- Outfit
- Performer used during dangerous scenes
- Spot where filming takes place

Arrange the circled letters to solve the mystery answer.

MYSTERY ANSWER

STARTS WITH F

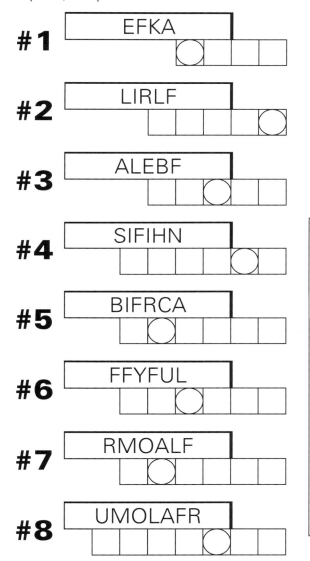

Unscramble the Jumbles, one letter to each square, to spell words that start with *F*.

#1 EFKA

#2 LIRLF

#3 ALEBF

#4 SIFIHN

#5 BIFRCA

#6 FFYFUL

#7 RMOALF

#8 UMOLAFR

JUMBLE BrainBusters

Box of Clues

Stumped? Maybe you can find a clue below.

-Symbolic expression of the chemical composition of a substance
-Story
-Material
-Not real
-Dressy
-End
-Wonderful
-Something decorative or useful and desirable but not essential
-Soft, airy

Arrange the circled letters to solve the mystery answer.

MYSTERY ANSWER

CITY, STATE

JUMBLE BrainBusters

Unscramble the Jumbles, one letter to each square, to spell names of cities and their corresponding U.S. states.

For example:

CITY
APAMT

STATE
DOFIALR

T A M P A , F L O R I D A

CITY

STATE

#1 LADASL

EXSAT

#2 AIMIM

RDFOIAL

#3 TAAALTN

AOIREGG

#4 EVERDN

DAOOCOLR

#5 NLAOTDPR

GOORNE

#6 RITETOD

AGIHNIMC

Arrange the circled letters to solve the mystery answers.

MYSTERY ANSWERS

CITY

STATE

FASHION

Unscramble the Jumbles, one letter to each square, to spell words related to fashion and clothing.

#1 RIHST

#2 RPAAK

#3 AEJSN

#4 ACRFS

#5 EJCATK

#6 TEINMT

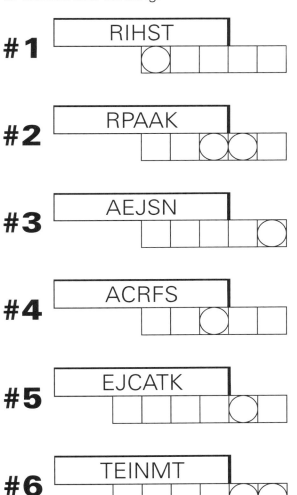

Interesting Fashion Facts

Toward the end of the 15th century, men's shoes had square tips.

The first alcohol-based perfumes were developed in the 1300s.

Arrange the circled letters to solve the mystery answer.

MYSTERY ANSWER

MATH

Unscramble the Jumbled
letters, one letter to each square,
so that each equation is correct.

For example: NONTEOEOW
O N E + O N E = T W O

#1 SIOSERIXZX

☐⊙☐ + ☐⊙☐☐ = ☐⊙☐

#2 EWFVHERETOIT

☐☐☐⊙ − ☐⊙☐☐ = ⊙☐☐

#3 WNVESIVTEOEF

☐☐☐☐⊙ − ☐☐☐⊙ = ☐☐☐

#4 EENITWNLEENVO

☐☐⊙☐ + ☐☐☐ = ☐☐☐☐☐⊙

#5 GFOROHUEITFUR

☐⊙☐☐ + ☐☐☐☐ = ☐☐⊙☐

Then arrange the
circled letters to solve
the mystery equation.

MYSTERY EQUATION

◯◯◯◯ + ◯◯◯◯◯◯ = ◯◯◯◯

TV SHOWS

Unscramble the Jumbles, one letter to each square, to spell names of TV shows.

JUMBLE BrainBusters

#1 APSO

#2 DUEAM

#3 RECESH

#4 NNACON

#5 EPFIRPL

#6 TRNHAWE

#7 DREPOYJA

Arrange the circled letters to solve the mystery answer.

Box of Clues

Stumped? Maybe you can find a clue below.

-NBC sitcom, 1982-1993
-TV sitcom, 1960-1972
-An *All in the Family* spin-off
-Popular TV game show
-Detective drama, 1971-1976
-Controversial sitcom, 1977-1981
-Long-running sitcom that shared its name with that of its star
-TV show starring a legless mammal

MYSTERY ANSWER

MEANS THE SAME

JUMBLE
BrainBusters

Unscramble the Jumbles, one letter
to each square, to spell pairs of words
that have the same or similar meanings.

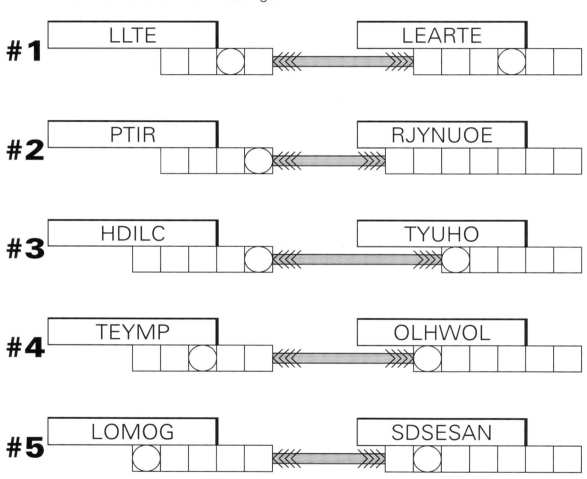

#1 LLTE   LEARTE

#2 PTIR   RJYNUOE

#3 HDILC   TYUHO

#4 TEYMP   OLHWOL

#5 LOMOG   SDSESAN

Arrange the circled letters to solve the mystery answer.
(Form two words that have the same or similar meanings.)

**MYSTERY
ANSWER**

WARS AND THE MILITARY

JUMBLE BrainBusters

Unscramble the Jumbles, one letter to each square, to spell words related to wars and the military.

#1 TUIN

#2 VAYN

#3 OMBB

#4 DRRAA

#5 OPEANW

#6 SISNIMO

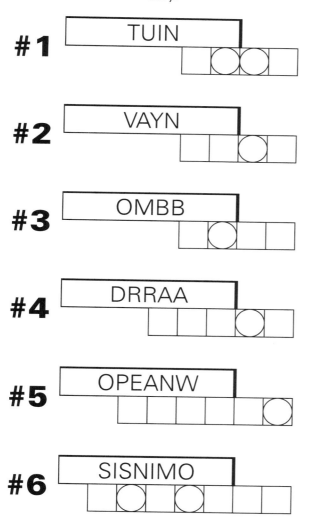

Box of Clues

Stumped? Maybe you can find a clue below.

- Starts with *M*; ends with *N*
- Starts with *R*; ends with *R*
- Starts with *I*; ends with *N*
- Starts with *U*; ends with *T*
- Starts with *B*; ends with *B*
- Starts with *N*; ends with *Y*
- Starts with *W*; ends with *N*

Arrange the circled letters to solve the mystery answer.

MYSTERY ANSWER

OCCUPATIONS

Unscramble the Jumbles, one letter to each square, to spell names of occupations.

#1 TARIEW

#2 NTOJIRA

#3 AREORTL

#4 RYUSVORE

#5 ACHYISINP

#6 RTNAEEPRC

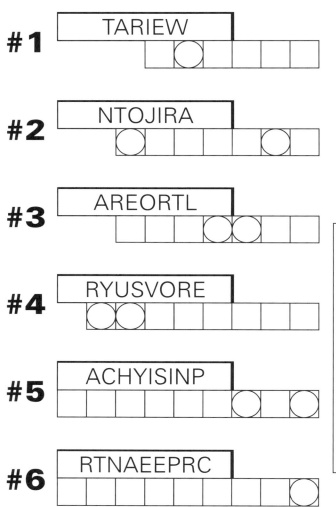

Box of Clues

Stumped? Maybe you can find a clue below.

- Starts with S; ends with R
- Starts with J; ends with R
- Starts with R; ends with R
- Starts with W; ends with R
- Starts with P; ends with N
- Starts with J; ends with T
- Starts with C; ends with R

Arrange the circled letters to solve the mystery answer.

MYSTERY ANSWER

MOVIES

Unscramble the Jumbles, one letter to each square, to spell names of movies.

#1 TATNPO

#2 RMIEYS

#3 OITOSET

#4 RHIEFMT

#5 BTEIRSDH

#6 NHGESTIT

#7 MTUHMYEM

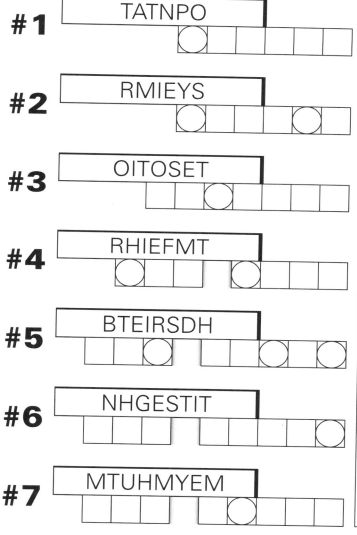

Box of Clues

Stumped? Maybe you can find a clue below.

- 1990 movie based on a Stephen King book
- 1982 Dustin Hoffman movie
- 1994 Tom Hanks movie
- 1973 movie starring Robert Redford and Paul Newman
- 1970 George C. Scott movie
- 1963 Alfred Hitchcock movie
- 1993 Tom Cruise movie based on a book
- 1999 Brendan Fraser movie

Arrange the circled letters to solve the mystery answer.

MYSTERY ANSWER

ADJECTIVES

JUMBLE BrainBusters

Unscramble the Jumbles, one letter to each square, to spell adjectives.

#1 RDIYT

#2 OFCYM

#3 NCDEET

#4 LBFYBA

#5 STFOYR

#6 LCUYMS

bright
sunny
warm

large
African
Asian

strong
muscular
powerful

Box of Clues

Stumped? Maybe you can find a clue below.

-Respectable
-Cold, icy
-Foul
-Powerful, compelling
-Awkward
-Cozy
-Out of shape

Arrange the circled letters to solve the mystery answer.

MYSTERY ANSWER

POETRY

JUMBLE BrainBusters

Unscramble the Jumbles, one letter to each square, to spell words found in the poem.

#1 ERGNDA

#2 RDLUYAN

#3 ANERSRD

#4 SESRST

#5 ADOTY

Procrastination
by Kim E. Nolan

The car needs to be washed
And the ____ #1 needs tending
There's ____ #2 to do
It's all never ending

There's dishes to do
And ____ #3 to run
I should take out the trash
But I'd rather have fun

I have a bad habit
It causes me ____ #4 and sorrow
I know what I should do ____ #5
But I'll wait until tomorrow

Arrange the circled letters to solve the mystery answer. (The mystery answer is not in the poem.)

MYSTERY ANSWER

WEATHER

**JUMBLE.
BrainBusters**

Unscramble the Jumbles, one letter to each square, to spell words related to weather.

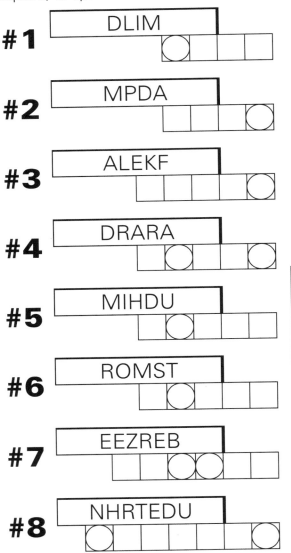

#1 DLIM

#2 MPDA

#3 ALEKF

#4 DRARA

#5 MIHDU

#6 ROMST

#7 EEZREB

#8 NHRTEDU

Arrange the circled letters to solve the mystery answer.

Interesting Weather Fact

According to NASA, the United States has the world's most violent weather. In a typical year, the United States can expect some 10,000 violent thunderstorms, 5,000 floods, 1,000 tornadoes, and several hurricanes.

MYSTERY ANSWER

ACTORS & ACTRESSES

JUMBLE
BrainBusters

Unscramble the Jumbles, one letter to each square, to spell names of actors and actresses.

#1 NDE YETABT

#2 TMO SREUIC

#3 LIWL HISMT

#4 LYIL LTINOM

#5 ALYSL LIDEF

#6 GRREO OMREO

Box of Clues

Stumped? Maybe you can find a clue below.

-*Enemy of the State* star
-*Minority Report* star
-*Moonraker* star
-*Nine to Five* star
-*Zelig* star
-*Kiss Me Goodbye* star
-*Deliverance* star

Arrange the circled letters to solve the mystery answer.

MYSTERY ANSWER

U.S. STATES

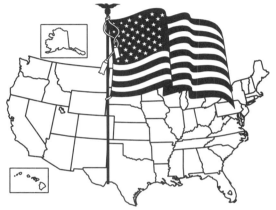

JUMBLE
BrainBusters

Unscramble the Jumbles, one letter to each square, to spell names of U.S. states.

#1 NAIME

#2 REGOAIG

#3 NWOGMIY

#4 ANMONAT

#5 SANEARBK

#6 RCLOOOAD

Arrange the circled letters to solve the mystery answer.

Box of Clues

Stumped? Maybe you can find a clue below.

-Home to Lincoln
-Largest state in New England
-Neighbor to Florida
-Home to Boulder
-U.S. state originally inhabited by Algonquian Indian tribes
-U.S. state that shares its name with a popular ex-quarterback
-Home to Gannett Peak (13,804 ft.)

MYSTERY ANSWER

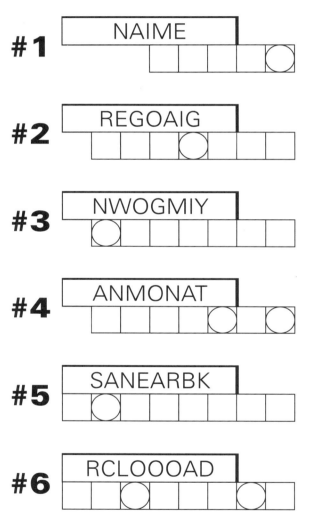

JUMBLE SPEAK

Unscramble the mixed up letters, one letter to each square, to spell words that will make complete sentences.

DDI   OYU   WNKO

ATHT   OMT   SURIEC

TLFE   ANRESIYM   HOSOLC

OT   CEEOBM   NA   TRCOA   ?

IST   RTEU   EH   PPREODD

UOT   TA   GAE   NAD   18

DEEHDA   OT   EWN   RYKO

YITC   OT   CTA

Arrange the circled letters to solve the mystery answer, which will relate to the subject of the "Jumble Speak."

MYSTERY ANSWER ○○○○ ○○○

U.S. PRESIDENTS

Unscramble the Jumbles, one letter
to each square, to spell the last names of
U.S. presidents.

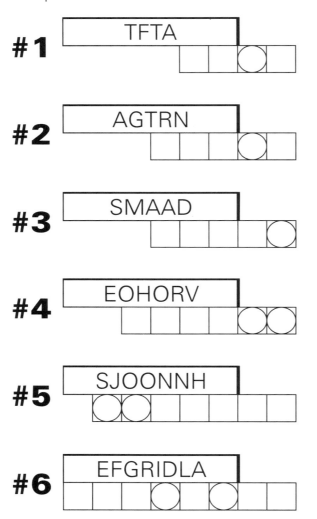

#1 TFTA

#2 AGTRN

#3 SMAAD

#4 EOHORV

#5 SJOONNH

#6 EFGRIDLA

Box of Clues

Stumped? Maybe you can find a clue
below.

-President who shared his name
 with a present-day fictional
 feline
-27th U.S. president
-17th or 36th U.S. president
-31st U.S. president
-John _____
-U.S. president born in
 Shadwell, Virginia
-President whose middle name
 was Simpson

Arrange the circled letters
to solve the mystery answer.

MYSTERY ANSWER

DOUBLE JUMBLE® BRAINBUSTERS

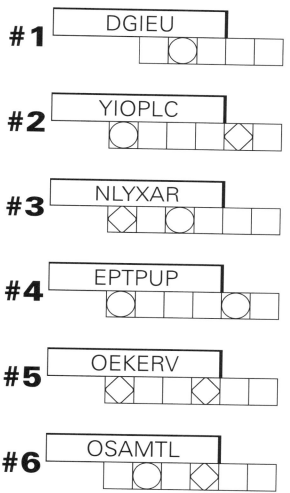

Unscramble the Jumbles, one letter to each square, to spell words.

#1 DGIEU

#2 YIOPLC

#3 NLYXAR

#4 EPTPUP

#5 OEKERV

#6 OSAMTL

JUMBLE BrainBusters

MYSTERY ANSWER #1 SUNNY
MYSTERY ANSWER #2 WEATHER

MYSTERY ANSWER #1 SPORTS
MYSTERY ANSWER #2 ATHLETES

MYSTERY ANSWER #1 COUNTRY
MYSTERY ANSWER #2 ETHIOPIA

Box of Clues

Stumped? Maybe you can find a clue below. (No clues for the mystery answers.)

-Rescind
-_____ dog
-Very near but not quite
-Insurance _____
-Hand _____
-Upper part of the trachea

Arrange the diamonded letters to solve mystery answer #1. Arrange the circled letters to solve mystery answer #2.
(The mystery answers will relate to each other.)

MYSTERY ANSWER #1

MYSTERY ANSWER #2

I LOVE LUCY

JUMBLE BrainBusters

Unscramble the Jumbles, one letter to each square, to spell words related to the television show *I Love Lucy*.

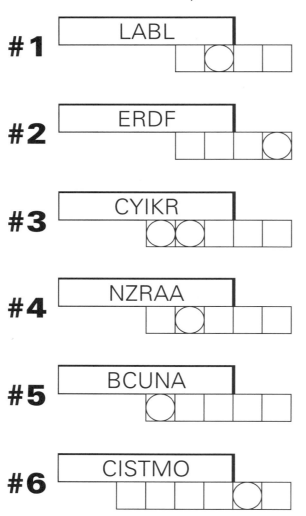

#1 LABL

#2 ERDF

#3 CYIKR

#4 NZRAA

#5 BCUNA

#6 CISTMO

Box of Clues

Stumped? Maybe you can find a clue below. (No clue for the mystery answer.)

-W.F. role
-Leading actress
-Leading actor
-Adjective that describes both Ricky and Desi
-"Little _____"
-Type of show

Arrange the circled letters to solve the mystery answer.

MYSTERY ANSWER

AROUND THE HOME

Unscramble the Jumbles, one letter
to each square, to spell words related
to the home.

#1 RCOHP

#2 NISIGD

#3 RTPAYN

#4 TUAECF

#5 AREGGA

Box of Clues

Stumped? Maybe you can find a clue
below. (No clue for the mystery answer.)

- Auto area
- Front _____
- System of pipes
- Flow regulator
- Exterior slats
- Small room or closet
- Smokestack

#6 MNHIYCE

#7 NBUIGPLM

Arrange the circled letters
to solve the mystery answer.

MYSTERY ANSWER

COUNTRIES

JUMBLE
BrainBusters

Unscramble the Jumbles, one letter to each square, to spell names of countries.

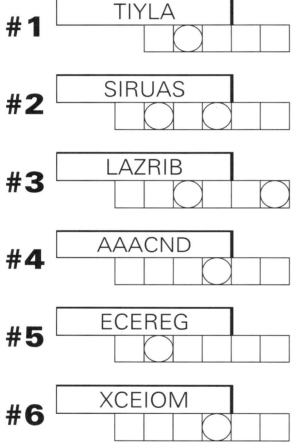

#1 TIYLA

#2 SIRUAS

#3 LAZRIB

#4 AAACND

#5 ECEREG

#6 XCEIOM

#7 ANIELDR

Box of Clues

Stumped? Maybe you can find a clue below.

-Starts with *G*; ends with *E*
-Starts with *R*; ends with *A*
-Starts with *I*; ends with *Y*
-Starts with *C*; ends with *A*
-Starts with *A*; ends with *A*
-Starts with *B*; ends with *L*
-Starts with *M*; ends with *O*
-Starts with *I*; ends with *D*

Arrange the circled letters to solve the mystery answer.

MYSTERY ANSWER

RHYMING WORDS

Unscramble the Jumbles, one letter
to each square, to spell pairs of words
that rhyme.

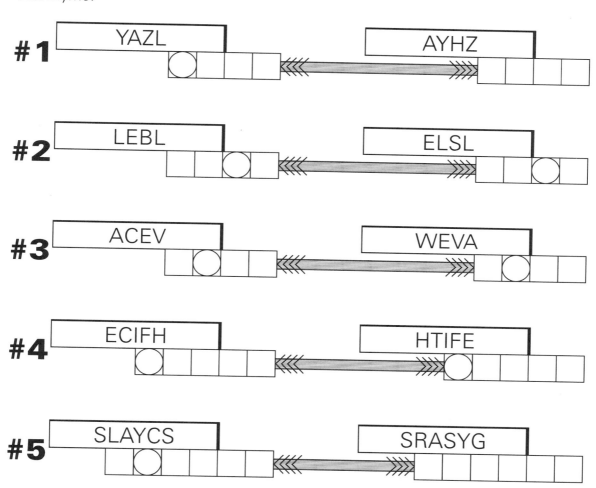

#1 YAZL   AYHZ

#2 LEBL   ELSL

#3 ACEV   WEVA

#4 ECIFH   HTIFE

#5 SLAYCS   SRASYG

Arrange the circled letters to solve the mystery answer.
(Form two words that rhyme.)

MYSTERY
ANSWER

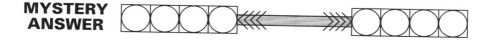

STATE CAPITALS

Unscramble the Jumbles, one letter to each square, to spell names of U.S. state capitals.

#1 TUINSA

#2 OSBNOT

#3 SLNNIAG

#4 NJCSOAK

#5 MBIACRKS

#6 LOONLUUH

Box of Clues

Stumped? Maybe you can find a clue below.

- Starts with *B*; ends with *N*
- Starts with *B*; ends with *K*
- Starts with *H*; ends with *U*
- Starts with *A*; ends with *N*
- Starts with *C*; ends with *S*
- Starts with *J*; ends with *N*
- Starts with *L*; ends with *G*

Arrange the circled letters to solve the mystery answer.

MYSTERY ANSWER

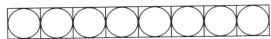

GOLF

JUMBLE BrainBusters

Unscramble the Jumbles, one letter to each square, to spell words related to golf.

#1 OHKO

#2 VDTIO

#3 GEELA

#4 DIRIBE

#5 LSDIEPM

#6 SRDESDA

#7 ATCLDSNO

#8 AGMLUINL

Box of Clues

Stumped? Maybe you can find a clue below.

- Two under par on a hole
- One under par on a hole
- The opposite of a slice
- Preparatory position of the player and club in golf
- Important annual tournament
- Ball indentations
- Loose piece of turf
- Free, extra shot
- Home to St. Andrews

Arrange the circled letters to solve the mystery answer.

MYSTERY ANSWER

DOUBLE CONSONANTS

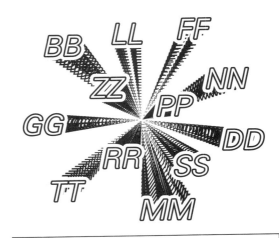

Unscramble the Jumbles, one letter to each square, to spell words that contain double consonants.

#1 BHYBU

#2 LAETRL

#3 EGLJGU

#4 FINFUM

#5 DILEMD

#6 OGLBEG

#7 LMEMUP

Arrange the circled letters to solve the mystery answer.

Box of Clues

Stumped? Maybe you can find a clue below.

-Handle or deal with usually several things at one time
-English _____
-Beat
-Muscular, short-haired mammal
-Center
-Everest to any other mountain on Earth
-Husband
-Confuse

MYSTERY ANSWER

GOING TO THE DENTIST

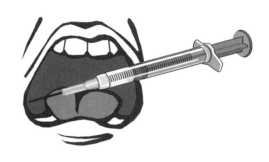

Unscramble the Jumbles, one letter to each square, to spell words related to going to the dentist.

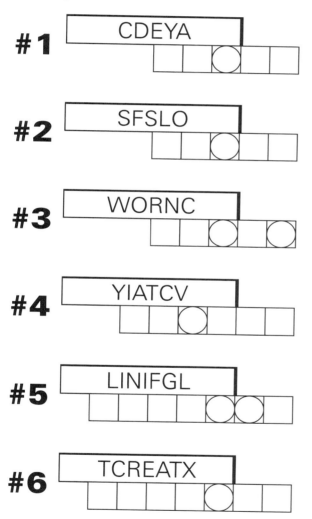

#1 CDEYA

#2 SFSLO

#3 WORNC

#4 YIATCV

#5 LINIFGL

#6 TCREATX

Box of Clues

Stumped? Maybe you can find a clue below. (No clue for the mystery answer.)

-Dental _____
-Destruction of the tooth
-Cavity fix
-Part of a tooth external to the gum or an artificial substitute for this
-Remove
-Area of decay in a tooth

Arrange the circled letters to solve the mystery answer.

MYSTERY ANSWER

FOOD & COOKING

Unscramble the Jumbles, one letter
to each square, to spell words related
to food and cooking.

#1 LRLIG

#2 HLNUC

#3 CASKN

#4 DUEGF

#5 AGIRCL

#6 ESHECE

#7 DERLNEB

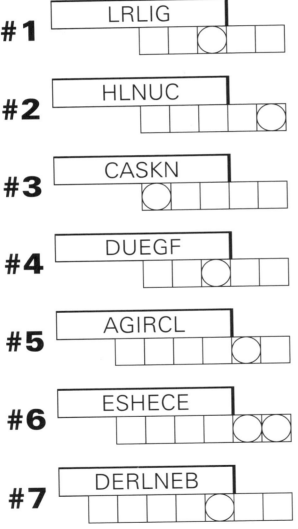

Arrange the circled letters
to solve the mystery answer.

Interesting Food Facts

It takes more calories to eat
and digest a piece of celery
than the celery has in it.

Olive oil is made from green
olives.

The average American eats
about 120 pounds of potatoes
each year.

MYSTERY ANSWER

ANIMALS

JUMBLE.
BrainBusters

Unscramble the Jumbles, one letter
to each square, to spell names of
animals.

#1 ELUM

#2 LEOM

#3 ANHEY

#4 OSOGE

#5 URTKYE

#6 AGORCU

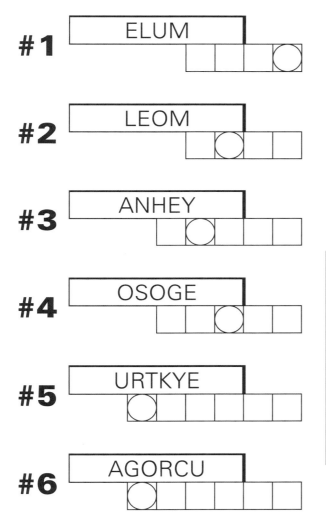

Interesting Animal Facts

Dinosaurs lived on Earth for
around 165 million years
before they became extinct.

A mole can dig a tunnel 300
feet long in one night.

Arrange the circled letters
to solve the mystery answer.

MYSTERY ANSWER

PLANET EARTH

Unscramble the Jumbles, one letter to each square, to spell words related to planet Earth.

#1 LFUBF

#2 SURTC

#3 ELOBG

#4 NAILDS

#5 OESANS

#6 ECLGRIA

#7 TQAREUO

Arrange the circled letters to solve the mystery answer.

Box of Clues

Stumped? Maybe you can find a clue below.

-Slow mover
-High, steep bank
-Barrier _____
-Earth's outer part
-Major source of oxygen
-A spherical representation
-Spring, for example
-Invisible middle

MYSTERY ANSWER

DOUBLE JUMBLE® BRAINBUSTERS

JUMBLE BrainBusters

Unscramble the Jumbles, one letter to each square, to spell words.

#1 DILIV

#2 GLUHA

#3 LFAEIN

#4 RHRDIO

#5 CAALEP

#6 SSLOYG

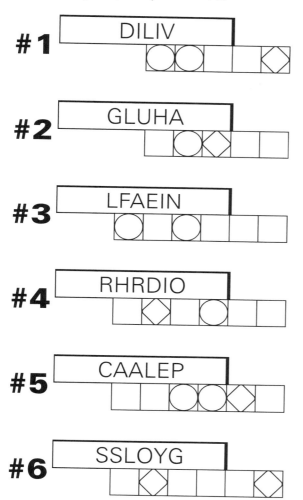

MYSTERY ANSWER #1 SUNNY
MYSTERY ANSWER #2 WEATHER

MYSTERY ANSWER #1 SPORTS
MYSTERY ANSWER #2 ATHLETES

MYSTERY ANSWER #1 COUNTRY
MYSTERY ANSWER #2 ETHIOPIA

Box of Clues

Stumped? Maybe you can find a clue below. (No clues for the mystery answers.)

-Buckingham _____
-Shiny
-Mad
-Giggle
-Shocking, inspiring disgust
-Ending

Arrange the diamonded letters to solve mystery answer #1. Arrange the circled letters to solve mystery answer #2. (The mystery answers will relate to each other.)

MYSTERY ANSWER #1

MYSTERY ANSWER #2

JUMBLE JOKES

Unscramble the mixed up letters to reveal the punch lines as suggested by the jokes.

#1 What runs around a baseball field but doesn't move?

NACEEF

#2 Why did the tree go to the dentist?

CNROTAALO

#3 What do bulls do when they go shopping?

GHEHARECTY

#4 What is a tornado's favorite game?

RSITEWT

#5 What do you call a cow sitting on dirt?

DERUNEFBGO

#6 What has three feet but can't walk?

CSAARTDIKY

#7 How much money does a skunk have?

NSONEETC

ADVERBS

Unscramble the Jumbles, one letter to each square, to spell adverbs.

#1 ASFYEL

#2 SIOLNIY

#3 LHIYTLG

#4 LFIREYB

#5 LRLEYCA

#6 SOELOYL

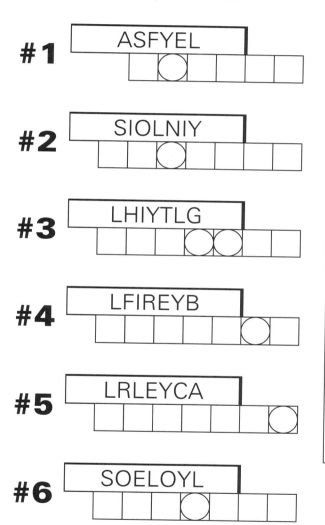

The runner ran <u>quickly</u>.
The runner ran <u>slowly</u>.

Box of Clues

Stumped? Maybe you can find a clue below.

-Loudly
-Unharmed
-With little weight or force
-In a hurried manner
-In a relaxed manner
-For a short time
-Without doubt or question

Arrange the circled letters to solve the mystery answer.

MYSTERY ANSWER

SUPER JUMBLE® CHALLENGE

JUMBLE. BrainBusters

#1 UFN

Unscramble the Jumbles, one letter to each square, to spell words.

#2 WHKA

#3 CTAKR

#4 UOTHRF

#5 PACOMTC

#6 NELGATPG

#7 ADGAIORTL

#8 EEINRDILCB

#9 CPLOIATINBU

#10 GDDIVATNAESA

Box of Clues
Stumped? Maybe you can find a clue below.

-Mars or April
-Glossy, edible fruit commonly used as a vegetable
-A bird of prey
-Newspaper or magazine
-Russell C.'s blockbuster
-_____ disc
-_____ airport
-Detriment
-Amazing
-_____ house
-Path

Arrange the circled letters to solve the mystery answer.

MYSTERY ANSWER

MUSICIANS

JUMBLE BrainBusters

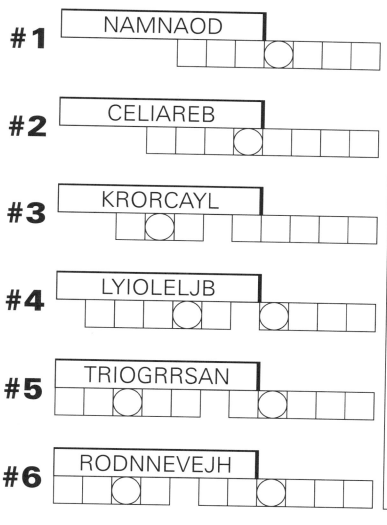

Unscramble the Jumbles, one letter to each square, to spell words related to occupations.

#1 NAMNAOD

#2 CELIAREB

#3 KRORCAYL

#4 LYIOLELJB

#5 TRIOGRRSAN

#6 RODNNEVEJH

Box of Clues

Stumped? Maybe you can find a clue below.

-Oldest Beatle
-Piano player and song writer born in the Bronx, New York, in 1949
-"Mr. Showmanship"
-Singer and actress born in Michigan in 1958
-Singer/songwriter born in England in 1947
-*Hee Haw* star
-Singer/songwriter who shared his last name with a U.S. city

Arrange the circled letters to solve the mystery answer.

MYSTERY ANSWER

STARTS WITH H

JUMBLE BrainBusters

Unscramble the Jumbles, one letter to each square, to spell words that start with *H*.

#1 BHITA

#2 OVHCA

#3 NUAMH

#4 EMHIRT

#5 LAGHGE

#6 AMHERM

#7 RHIUCTA

#8 TSHAERM

Arrange the circled letters to solve the mystery answer.

Box of Clues

Stumped? Maybe you can find a clue below.

-Small rodent
-Construction tool
-Great confusion and disorder
-A reason to take a seat
-Force of _____
-Person
-Legacy, tradition
-Wrangle
-_____ crab

MYSTERY ANSWER

ANIMALS

Unscramble the Jumbles, one letter to each square, to spell names of animals.

#1 OAKAL

#2 NEIOGP

#3 AUJARG

#4 ROGHEP

#5 LEASWE

#6 LAUSRW

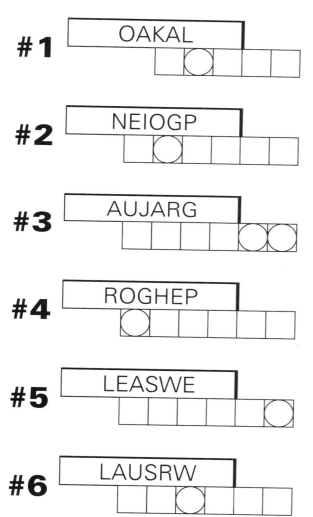

Box of Clues

Stumped? Maybe you can find a clue below.

-Large cat of Central and South America
-Small, slender carnivore
-Burrowing rodent
-Mountain _____
-Australian marsupial
-Large marine mammal
-City bird

Arrange the circled letters to solve the mystery answer.

MYSTERY ANSWER

COUNTRIES

Unscramble the Jumbles, one letter to each square, to spell names of countries.

#1 BCUA

#2 DIAIN

#3 ARNEFC

#4 RNOAYW

#5 VIOILAB

#6 LDAIFNN

#7 MEDUABR

Box of Clues

Stumped? Maybe you can find a clue below.

- Neighbor to Pakistan
- Home to Helsinki
- Brazil's western neighbor
- Country with coasts on the Mediterranean and Atlantic
- Island country in the West Indies
- Island associated with a shape
- The world's largest producer of emeralds
- Home to Oslo

Arrange the circled letters to solve the mystery answer.

MYSTERY ANSWER

CITY, STATE

JUMBLE BrainBusters

Unscramble the Jumbles, one letter to each square, to spell names of cities and their corresponding U.S. states.

For example:

CITY
APAMT

STATE
DOFIALR

TAMPA, FLORIDA

CITY — **STATE**

#1 ANUUJE — LAAKAS

#2 SOOUHNT — TASEX

#3 BLOIME — MALAAAB

#4 NXHEIPO — NRAAIOZ

#5 DOLAONR — AFIRODL

#6 NAOTDPLR — GRENOO

MYSTERY ANSWERS

Arrange the circled letters to solve the mystery answers.

CITY ⬭⬭⬭⬭⬭, STATE ⬭⬭⬭⬭⬭

BIRDS

Unscramble the Jumbles, one letter to each square, to spell words related to birds.

#1 OIRNB

#2 RTSKO

#3 SOGEO

#4 EOPING

#5 KTYUER

#6 AYCRAN

#7 COTHRIS

#8 NFLGMIOA

Box of Clues

Stumped? Maybe you can find a clue below.

- Starts with *C*; ends with *Y*
- Starts with *S*; ends with *K*
- Starts with *R*; ends with *N*
- Starts with *P*; ends with *N*
- Starts with *P*; ends with *T*
- Starts with *O*; ends with *H*
- Starts with *T*; ends with *Y*
- Starts with *F*; ends with *O*
- Starts with *G*; ends with *E*

Arrange the circled letters to solve the mystery answer.

MYSTERY ANSWER

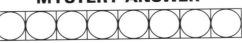

BUILDING A HOUSE

Unscramble the Jumbles, one letter to each square, to spell words related to building a house.

#1 SIJTO

#2 MIEPTR

#3 NIRIWG

#4 TCNEEM

#5 MRAEHM

#6 YDOPOLW

#7 NIWSWOD

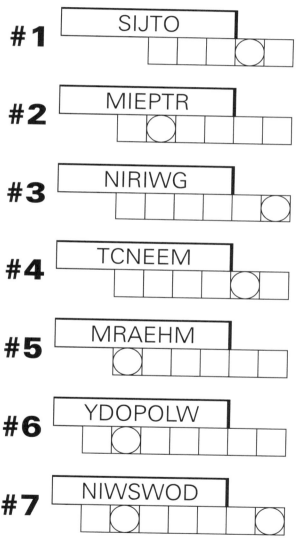

Box of Clues

Stumped? Maybe you can find a clue below. (No clue for the mystery answer.)

- Building material that comes in a sheet
- Powder of alumina, silica, lime, iron oxide, and magnesium oxide
- Building _____
- Floor _____
- Transparent units
- Electric system connections
- Pounding tool

Arrange the circled letters to solve the mystery answer.

MYSTERY ANSWER

RHYMING WORDS

Unscramble the Jumbles, one letter
to each square, to spell pairs of words
that rhyme.

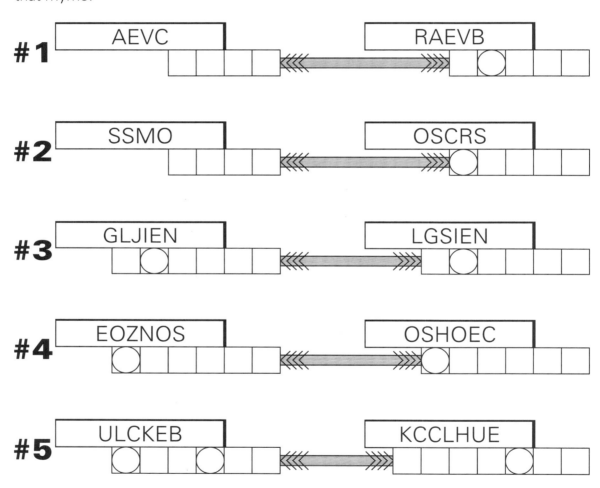

#1 AEVC — RAEVB

#2 SSMO — OSCRS

#3 GLJIEN — LGSIEN

#4 EOZNOS — OSHOEC

#5 ULCKEB — KCCLHUE

Arrange the circled letters to solve the mystery answer.
(Form two words that rhyme.)

**MYSTERY
ANSWER**

OUTER SPACE

Unscramble the Jumbles, one letter to each square, to spell words related to outer space.

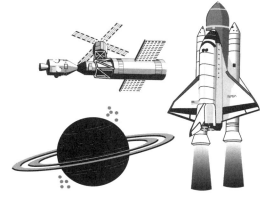

#1 MCTOE

#2 NUSAUR

#3 YXAALG

#4 OLAOLP

#5 PNNUEET

#6 CEUMYRR

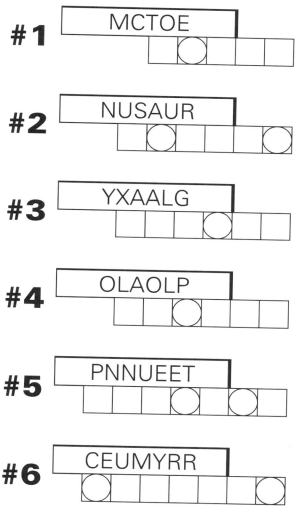

Box of Clues

Stumped? Maybe you can find a clue below.

- Tailed orbiter
- Famous NASA missions
- Saturn's outer neighbor
- Home to Triton (a very large moon)
- One of Galileo's passions
- Large collection of stars and planets
- Dry, rocky planet

Arrange the circled letters to solve the mystery answer.

MYSTERY ANSWER

MOVIES

JUMBLE
BrainBusters

Unscramble the Jumbles, one letter
to each square, to spell names of movies.

#1 ENAISL

#2 NOGUPT

#3 TIREGVO

#4 FRICTFA

#5 HADERID

#6 GIGKNKON

#7 NIOHGHNO

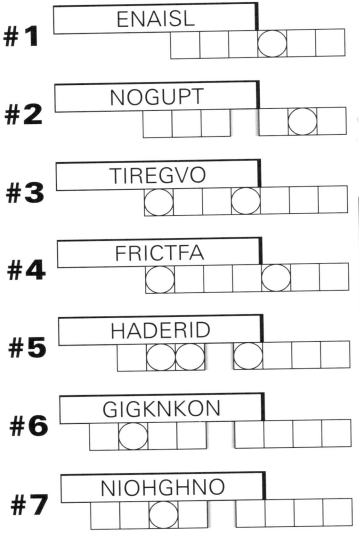

Box of Clues

Stumped? Maybe you can find
a clue below.

- 1986 Tom Cruise movie
- 1986 Sigourney Weaver
  movie set in outer space
- 1952 Western
- 1988 Bruce Willis movie
- 2000 Michael Douglas
  movie
- 1993 Harrison Ford
  movie
- 1933 monster movie
- 1958 Jimmy Stewart
  movie

Arrange the circled
letters to solve the
mystery answer.

MYSTERY ANSWER

ALL ABOUT MUSIC

Unscramble the Jumbles, one letter to each square, to spell words related to music.

#1 SOGN

#2 NIOPA

#3 RCDOH

#4 MURSD

#5 EOPTM

#6 ATGIRU

#7 ROETNC

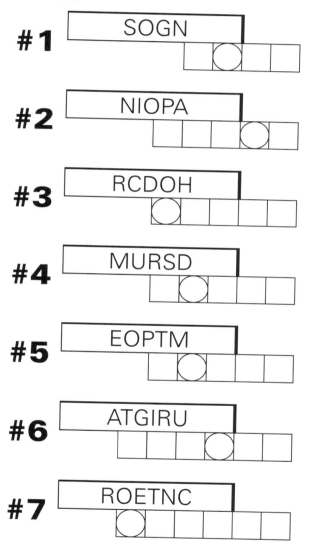

Interesting Music Facts

Bette Midler's 1971 album, *The Divine Miss M*, was produced by Barry Manilow.

Irving Berlin wrote more than 900 songs, 19 musicals, and the musical scores of 18 movies.

Arrange the circled letters to solve the mystery answer.

MYSTERY ANSWER

MEANS THE OPPOSITE

JUMBLE BrainBusters

Unscramble the Jumbles, one letter to each square, to spell pairs of words that have opposite or nearly opposite meanings.

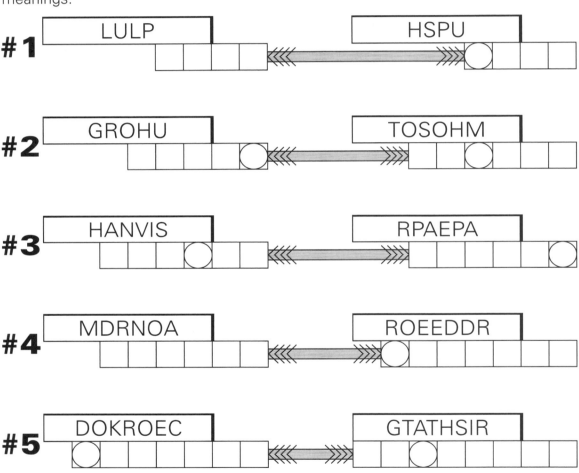

#1 LULP — HSPU

#2 GROHU — TOSOHM

#3 HANVIS — RPAEPA

#4 MDRNOA — ROEEDDR

#5 DOKROEC — GTATHSIR

Arrange the circled letters to solve the mystery answer. (Form two words that have the opposite or nearly opposite meanings.)

MYSTERY ANSWER

DOUBLE JUMBLE® BRAINBUSTERS

JUMBLE.
BrainBusters

Unscramble the Jumbles, one letter to each square, to spell words.

#1 OVSEH

#2 TPIUDR

#3 EAGLGG

#4 FCEOEF

#5 GOJRNA

#6 RWSLPA

MYSTERY ANSWER #1 S U N N Y
MYSTERY ANSWER #2 W E A T H E R

MYSTERY ANSWER #1 S P O R T S
MYSTERY ANSWER #2 A T H L E T E S

MYSTERY ANSWER #1 C O U N T R Y
MYSTERY ANSWER #2 E T H I O P I A

Box of Clues

Stumped? Maybe you can find a clue below. (No clues for the mystery answers.)

-Black _____
-Urban _____
-Push
-Flock of geese
-Terminology, dialect
-Rotten

Arrange the diamonded letters to solve mystery answer #1. Arrange the circled letters to solve mystery answer #2.
(The mystery answers will relate to each other.)

MYSTERY ANSWER #1

MYSTERY ANSWER #2

THE HUMAN BODY

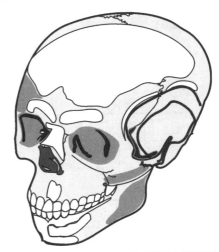

Unscramble the Jumbles, one letter to each square, to spell words related to the human body.

#1 ARINB

#2 NLEAK

#3 LOBDO

#4 LEISVP

#5 NEIYKD

#6 MEELNA

#7 MDERRAU

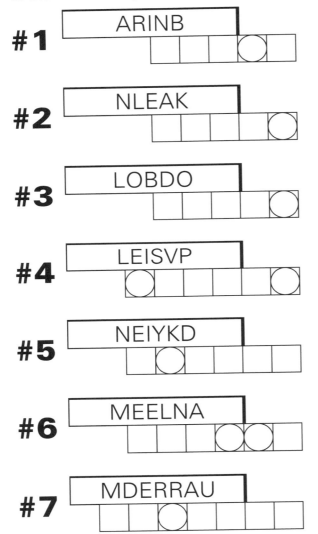

Box of Clues

Stumped? Maybe you can find a clue below.

- Starts with *K*; ends with *Y*
- Starts with *P*; ends with *S*
- Starts with *E*; ends with *S*
- Starts with *A*; ends with *E*
- Starts with *B*; ends with *N*
- Starts with *B*; ends with *D*
- Starts with *E*; ends with *L*
- Starts with *E*; ends with *M*

Arrange the circled letters to solve the mystery answer.

MYSTERY ANSWER

MEANS THE SAME

JUMBLE
BrainBusters

Unscramble the Jumbles, one letter
to each square, to spell pairs of words
that have the same or similar meanings.

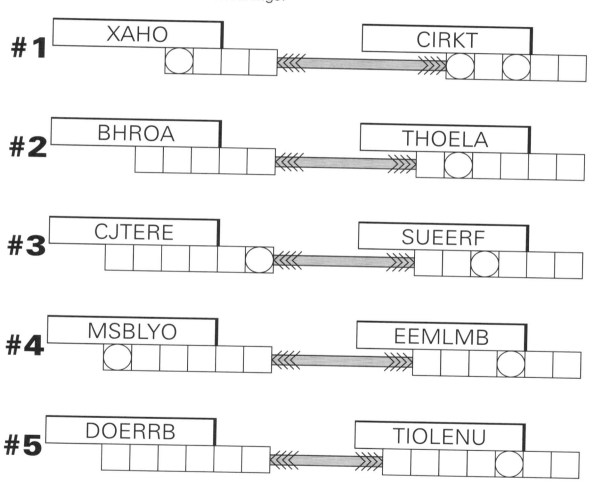

#1 XAHO — CIRKT

#2 BHROA — THOELA

#3 CJTERE — SUEERF

#4 MSBLYO — EEMLMB

#5 DOERRB — TIOLENU

Arrange the circled letters to solve the mystery answer.
(Form two words that have the same or similar meanings.)

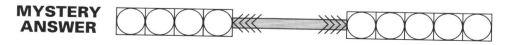

**MYSTERY
ANSWER**

WARS AND THE MILITARY

JUMBLE BrainBusters

Unscramble the Jumbles, one letter to each square, to spell words related to wars and the military.

#1 SAEB ◯◯

#2 MROAR ◯

#3 EUBTLL ◯

#4 CEETFD ◯ ◯

#5 FEFRICO ◯

#6 ARTENEV ◯ ◯

Interesting Military Facts

Actor Jimmy Stewart attained the rank of brigadier general in the U.S. Air Force Reserve, the highest U.S. military rank in history for an entertainer.

"Soldiers' disease" was a term used to describe Civil War soldiers who became addicted to morphine.

Arrange the circled letters to solve the mystery answer.

MYSTERY ANSWER
◯◯◯◯◯◯◯◯◯

ALL ABOUT MONEY

JUMBLE BrainBusters

Unscramble the Jumbles, one letter to each square, to spell words related to money.

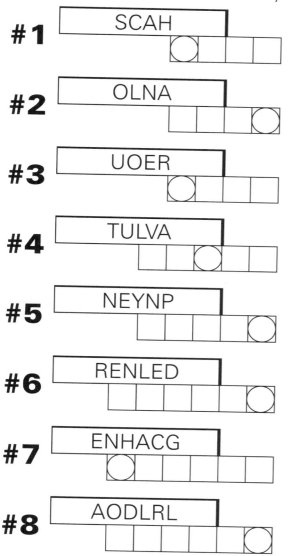

#1 SCAH

#2 OLNA

#3 UOER

#4 TULVA

#5 NEYNP

#6 RENLED

#7 ENHACG

#8 AODLRL

Arrange the circled letters to solve the mystery answer.

Box of Clues

Stumped? Maybe you can find a clue below.

-Home or car _____
-A.L.'s coin
-_____ register
-Secure area
-Circulation as a medium of exchange
-Finance company
-Loose or pocket _____
-Canadian or U.S. _____
-E.U. currency

MYSTERY ANSWER

SPORTS

JUMBLE BrainBusters

Unscramble the Jumbles, one letter to each square, to spell words related to sports.

#1 NISKIG

#2 PRIELT

#3 XNBIGO

#4 TAPNLYE

#5 SFONEEF

#6 FYALFOP

Box of Clues

Stumped? Maybe you can find a clue below. (No clue for the mystery answer.)

- Quarterback's or pitcher's side
- Snow _____
- One on one sport
- Game or series played after the end of the regular season
- Type of baseball hit
- Reason for a ref to blow the whistle

Arrange the circled letters to solve the mystery answer.

MYSTERY ANSWER

"COLORFUL" WORDS

JUMBLE BrainBusters

Unscramble the Jumbles, one letter to each square, to spell words that have a color in their name, as shown in the examples.

Examples:

REDUCE

BLUEBIRD

BLACKBIRD

WHITEWALL

#1 SHDGOILF

#2 KUOBCTAL

#3 ARMCEYRE

#4 PLTURNBIE

#5 ECBEANKRG

#6 SWRONOBTE

Box of Clues

Stumped? Maybe you can find a clue below. (No clue for the mystery answer.)

- Plan
- Type of building
- Nickname for money from the United States
- Establishment where butter and cheese are produced
- Creature that lives in water
- Reason to get a candle or a flashlight

Arrange the circled letters to solve the mystery answer.

MYSTERY ANSWER

COMPUTERS

Unscramble the Jumbles, one letter to each square, to spell words related to computers.

#1 TYEB

#2 NEUM

#3 UIRVS

#4 DOMME

#5 PTLOPA

#6 OMARTF

#7 RMPROAG

#8 RNITEENT

Arrange the circled letters to solve the mystery answer.

Box of Clues

Stumped? Maybe you can find a clue below.

-Starts with *V*; ends with *S*
-Starts with *F*; ends with *T*
-Starts with *B*; ends with *E*
-Starts with *M*; ends with *U*
-Starts with *P*; ends with *M*
-Starts with *M*; ends with *M*
-Starts with *D*; ends with *E*
-Starts with *I*; ends with *T*
-Starts with *L*; ends with *P*

MYSTERY ANSWER

STARTS WITH AND ENDS WITH A VOWEL

JUMBLE BrainBusters

Unscramble the Jumbles, one letter to each square, to spell words that start with and end with a vowel.

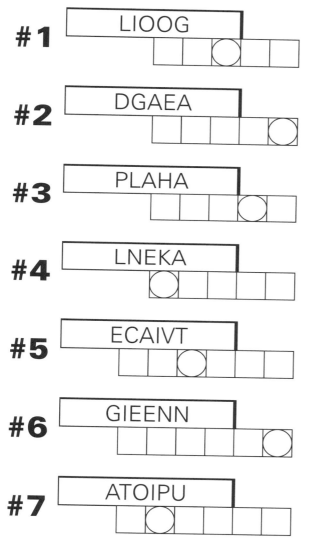

#1 LIOOG

#2 DGAEA

#3 PLAHA

#4 LNEKA

#5 ECAIVT

#6 GIEENN

#7 ATOIPU

Arrange the circled letters to solve the mystery answer.

Box of Clues

Stumped? Maybe you can find a clue below.

-Lower joint
-Busy
-Saying
-Type of competitor
-Power source
-Northern home
-The first of its kind
-Place of ideal perfection

MYSTERY ANSWER

RHYMES WITH . . .

Unscramble the Jumbles, one letter
to each square, to spell words that will
each have a corresponding rhyming clue.

#1 KCHIT

#2 TCAHP

#3 KSKNU

#4 SUGSE

#5 EHYNO

#6 OWRNC

#7 RTCTESA

Arrange the circled letters
to solve the mystery answer.

TON - - - FUN
BACK - - - STACK
TRUCK - - - STUCK
MISTER - - - SISTER

Box of Clues

Stumped? Maybe you can find a clue
below.

-Rhymes with *funny*
-Rhymes with *match*
-Rhymes with *trunk*
-Rhymes with *less*
-Rhymes with *stick*
-Rhymes with *butter*
-Rhymes with *brown*
-Rhymes with *matter*

MYSTERY ANSWER

PUZZLE 60

GOING ON A CRUISE

Unscramble the Jumbles, one letter to each square, to spell words related to going on a cruise.

#1 KODC

#2 ERWC

#3 NICSOA

#4 SEESLV

#5 LEAGYL

#6 TFBEFU

#7 OAYGVE

#8 TAICANP

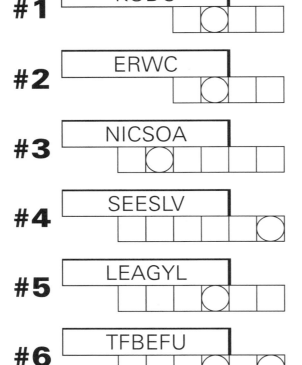

Box of Clues

Stumped? Maybe you can find a clue below.

-Whole company belonging to a ship sometimes including the officers and master
-Journey
-Ship kitchen area
-Stop included on an itinerary
-Platform for the loading or unloading of passengers and materials
-Ship gaming area
-Food service style common on a cruise
-Ship
-Person in charge of the ship

Arrange the circled letters to solve the mystery answer.

MYSTERY ANSWER

FIRST OF ITS KIND

Unscramble the Jumbles, one letter to each square, to spell names of things that are considered to be the first of their kind.

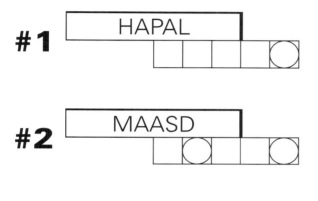

#1 HAPAL

#2 MAASD

#3 RAJAYNU

#4 CEYRUMR

#5 RHEDOYNG

Box of Clues

Stumped? Maybe you can find a clue below. (No clue for the mystery answer.)

-The first of nine
-The first U.S. vice president
-The first Greek letter
-The most abundant element and the first element on the table of elements
-The first of 12

Arrange the circled letters to solve the mystery answer.

MYSTERY ANSWER

OCCUPATIONS

Unscramble the Jumbles, one letter to each square, to spell names of occupations.

#1 TOILP

#2 SRUEN

#3 ACOHC

#4 RBARBE

#5 REEJELW

#6 BUELMRP

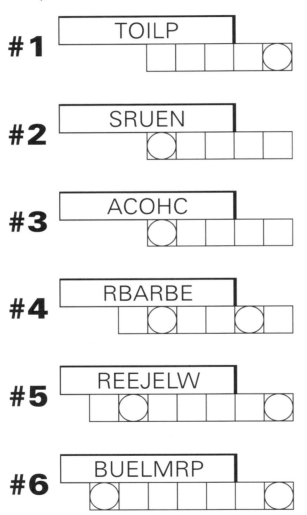

Box of Clues

Stumped? Maybe you can find a clue below.

-Starts with *J*; ends with *R*
-Starts with *C*; ends with *R*
-Starts with *B*; ends with *R*
-Starts with *N*; ends with *E*
-Starts with *P*; ends with *T*
-Starts with *P*; ends with *R*
-Starts with *C*; ends with *H*

Arrange the circled letters to solve the mystery answer.

MYSTERY ANSWER

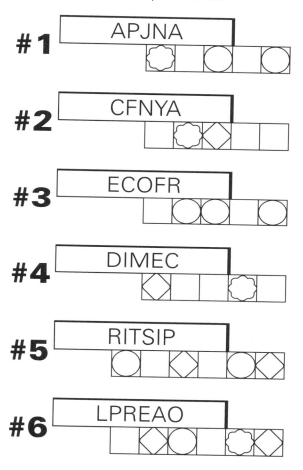

TRIPLE JUMBLE® BRAINBUSTERS

Unscramble the Jumbles, one letter to each square, to spell words.

#1 APJNA

#2 CFNYA

#3 ECOFR

#4 DIMEC

#5 RITSIP

#6 LPREAO

JUMBLE BrainBusters

MYSTERY ANSWER #1 CHEF
MYSTERY ANSWER #2 BROIL
MYSTERY ANSWER #3 SEAFOOD

MYSTERY ANSWER #1 FISH
MYSTERY ANSWER #2 TROUT
MYSTERY ANSWER #3 UPSTREAM

Box of Clues

Stumped? Maybe you can find a clue below. (No clues for the mystery answers.)

- _____ officer
- Asian country
- Air _____
- Extravagant
- Doctor
- Ghost

Arrange the clouded letters to solve mystery answer #1. Arrange the diamonded letters to solve mystery answer #2. Arrange the circled letters to solve mystery answer #3.

(The mystery answers will relate to each other.)

MYSTERY ANSWER #1

MYSTERY ANSWER #2

MYSTERY ANSWER #3

ENDS IN I

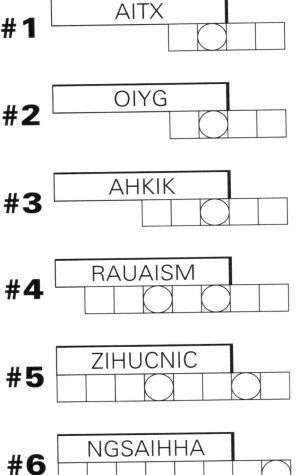

Unscramble the Jumbles, one letter to each square, to spell words that end in *I*.

#1 AITX

#2 OIYG

#3 AHKIK

#4 RAUAISM

#5 ZIHUCNIC

#6 NGSAIHHA

Arrange the circled letters to solve the mystery answer.

MIAMI   SAFARI
GANDHI   BIKINI

Ends in "I"

GEMINI   ALKALI
TAHITI
SCAMPI   HAITI

Box of Clues

Stumped? Maybe you can find a clue below. (No clue for the mystery answer.)

-_____ warrior
-Asian city
-Summer squash of bushy growth with smooth, cylindrical, usually dark green fruit
-Markedly reflective or mystical person
-Light yellowish brown
-Cab

MYSTERY ANSWER

ELEMENTS

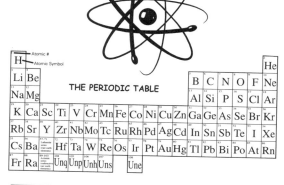

Unscramble the Jumbles, one letter
to each square, to spell names of
elements.

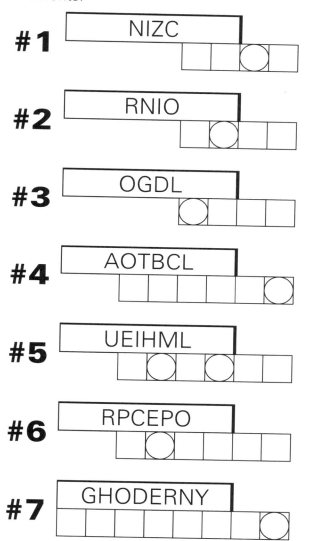

#1 NIZC

#2 RNIO

#3 OGDL

#4 AOTBCL

#5 UEIHML

#6 RPCEPO

#7 GHODERNY

Arrange the circled letters
to solve the mystery answer.

Box of Clues

Stumped? Maybe you can find a clue
below.

-Starts with *C*; ends with *T*
-Starts with *G*; ends with *D*
-Starts with *H*; ends with *M*
-Starts with *Z*; ends with *C*
-Starts with *N*; ends with *N*
-Starts with *C*; ends with *R*
-Starts with *H*; ends with *N*
-Starts with *I*; ends with *N*

MYSTERY ANSWER

CITY, COUNTRY

JUMBLE BrainBusters

Unscramble the Jumbles, one letter to each square, to spell names of cities and their corresponding countries.

For example:

CITY
NOORTOT
TORONTO,

COUNTRY
NCAAAD
CANADA

CITY

COUNTRIES

#1 LIAM — REUP

#2 OMER — ATIYL

#3 RACIO — GETYP

#4 ABMBOY — NIAID

#5 ARWSWA — NPDOAL

#6 ONOTOTR — ACNAAD

Arrange the circled letters to solve the mystery answers.

MYSTERY ANSWERS

CITY ⎯⎯⎯⎯⎯⎯, COUNTRY ⎯⎯⎯⎯⎯

ADJECTIVES

JUMBLE BrainBusters

Unscramble the Jumbles, one letter to each square, to spell adjectives.

#1 HFSIY

#2 EIEER

#3 NUFYN

#4 RFUYR

#5 TPYME

#6 HGBITR

#7 BRBAYC

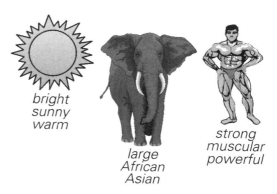

bright
sunny
warm

large
African
Asian

strong
muscular
powerful

Box of Clues

Stumped? Maybe you can find a clue below.

- Amusing
- Adjective that can describe a rabbit
- Smart
- Timesaving
- Grumpy
- Creating doubt or suspicion
- Mysterious
- Hollow

Arrange the circled letters to solve the mystery answer.

MYSTERY ANSWER

U.S. PRESIDENTS

Unscramble the Jumbles, one letter to each square, to spell the last names of U.S. presidents.

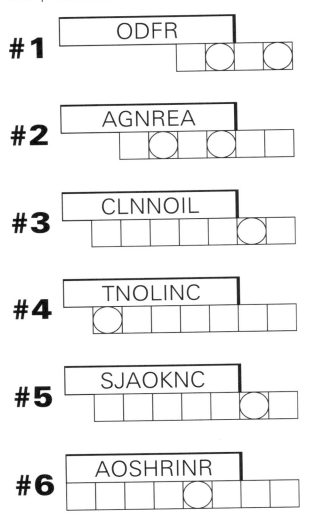

#1 ODFR

#2 AGNREA

#3 CLNNOIL

#4 TNOLINC

#5 SJAOKNC

#6 AOSHRINR

Interesting Presidential Facts

John Adams was the first president to live in the White House.

President William McKinley always wore a red carnation in his lapel for good luck.

Ulysses S. Grant was the first president whose parents were both alive when he was inaugurated.

Arrange the circled letters to solve the mystery answer.

MYSTERY ANSWER

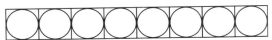

TV SHOWS

JUMBLE BrainBusters

Unscramble the Jumbles, one letter to each square, to spell names of TV shows.

#1 RTEUNH

#2 AFILYM

#3 NENOSB

#4 RFIEARS

#5 TDYSYAN

#6 OTCAMKL

#7 BUCOOML

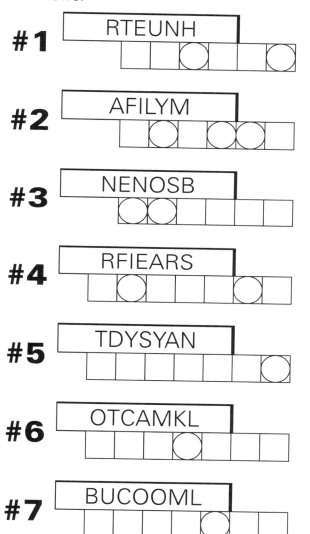

Box of Clues

Stumped? Maybe you can find a clue below.

- P.F. police drama
- *Soap* spin-off
- Long-running nighttime soap
- A.G. legal drama
- ABC sitcom, 1975-1982
- F.D. police drama
- ABC drama, 1976-1980
- *Cheers* spin-off

Arrange the circled letters to solve the mystery answer.

MYSTERY ANSWER

DOUBLE JUMBLE® BRAINBUSTERS

Unscramble the Jumbles, one letter to each square, to spell words.

#1 EDUSE

#2 SAINIR

#3 NSRIKH

#4 LADLSA

#5 GULEEA

#6 LBHUEM

JUMBLE® BrainBusters

MYSTERY ANSWER #1 SUNNY
MYSTERY ANSWER #2 WEATHER

MYSTERY ANSWER #1 SPORTS
MYSTERY ANSWER #2 ATHLETES

MYSTERY ANSWER #1 COUNTRY
MYSTERY ANSWER #2 ETHIOPIA

Box of Clues

Stumped? Maybe you can find a clue below. (No clues for the mystery answers.)

-Modest
-Dried grape
-Leather with a napped surface
-Little or major _____
-A large U.S. city
-Reduce

Arrange the diamonded letters to solve mystery answer #1. Arrange the circled letters to solve mystery answer #2.
(The mystery answers will relate to each other.)

MYSTERY ANSWER #1

MYSTERY ANSWER #2

ALL ABOUT HORSES

Unscramble the Jumbles, one letter to each square, to spell words related to horses.

#1 OHOF

#2 RMFA

#3 LTSLA

#4 DNASH

#5 DSLAED

#6 OKJCEY

#7 BARINAA

#8 DCDOPKA

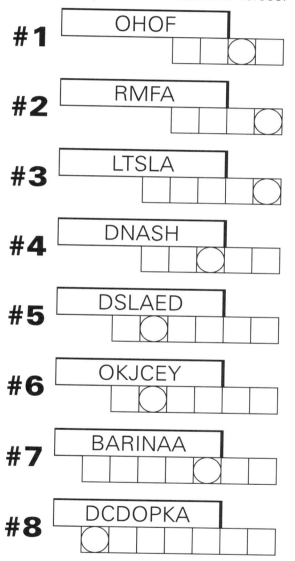

Box of Clues

Stumped? Maybe you can find a clue below.

- Rider
- Plot of land where horses are often found
- Horse compartment
- Measurement units
- Horse that is pale cream to gold in color and has a flaxen or white mane and tail
- Swift, compact horse
- Enclosure where racehorses are saddled
- Foot
- Padded seat

Arrange the circled letters to solve the mystery answer.

MYSTERY ANSWER

WORLD SERIES WINNERS

JUMBLE. BrainBusters

Unscramble the Jumbles, one letter to each square, to spell names of baseball teams that have won the World Series.

#1 RDES

#2 NISWT

#3 RGIEST

#4 SAERVB

#5 ENAYESK

#6 NLIARSM

#7 OEDRSGD

#8 LDAINASCR

Box of Clues

Stumped? Maybe you can find a clue below.

#1) 1990 World Series winner
#2) 1987 World Series winner
#3) 1984 World Series winner
#4) 1995 World Series winner
#5) 1996 World Series winner
#6) 1997 World Series winner
#7) 1988 World Series winner
#8) 1982 World Series winner
M.A.) 2001 Word Series winner

Arrange the circled letters to solve the mystery answer.

MYSTERY ANSWER

M*A*S*H

JUMBLE BrainBusters

#1 DAAL

#2 OEKAR

#3 DARRA

#4 JOARM

#5 TORETP

#6 RGLNIEK

#7 PACNITA

#8 RPRTEAP

#9 STOODRC

Unscramble the Jumbles, one letter to each square, to spell words related to the television show *M*A*S*H*.

Box of Clues

Stumped? Maybe you can find a clue below. (No clue for the mystery answer.)

-W.R. role
-"Hot Lips" rank
-Alan _____
-Hunnicut's rank
-J.F. role
-Setting
-G.B. role
-Surgeons
-H.M. role

Arrange the circled letters to solve the mystery answer.

MYSTERY ANSWER

FOOD & COOKING

Unscramble the Jumbles, one letter to each square, to spell words related to food and cooking.

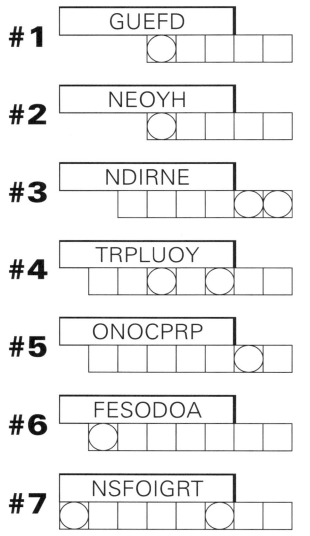

#1 GUEFD

#2 NEOYH

#3 NDIRNE

#4 TRPLUOY

#5 ONOCPRP

#6 FESODOA

#7 NSFOIGRT

Arrange the circled letters to solve the mystery answer.

Box of Clues

Stumped? Maybe you can find a clue below.

-Fried clams
-Sweet coating
-Chicken or turkey
-Buttered _____
-Sweet, viscid material
-An apple that's just been picked
-Late afternoon or early evening meal
-Creamy candy

MYSTERY ANSWER

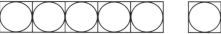 

ANIMAL GROUPINGS

Unscramble the Jumbles, one letter to each square, to spell names of animals.

#1 WCOSR

#2 NAHESY

#3 AERSBZ

#4 EAHWSL

#5 EUTRYSK

#6 GRAESBD

#7 NSDHIPOL

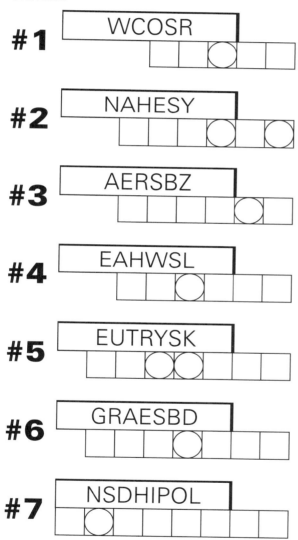

Box of Clues
Stumped? Maybe you can find a clue below.

#1) A group of these is called a murder

#2) A group of these is called a clan

#3) A group of these is called a zeal

#4) A group of these is called a school or herd

#5) A group of these is called a rafter, gang, or muster

#6) A group of these is called a cete

#7) A group of these is called a school

M.A.) A group of these is called a mob or troop

Arrange the circled letters to solve the mystery answer.

MYSTERY ANSWER

SUPER JUMBLE® CHALLENGE

JUMBLE. BrainBusters

#1 FGO

Unscramble the Jumbles, one letter to each square, to spell words.

#2 OLKO

#3 LCKIC

#4 HORTYP

#5 NCAAEBL

#6 DIHYUITM

#7 CIFTEINNO

#8 NSTALPATRN

#9 TPSEIOIHCRR

#10 TLINEULETALC

Box of Clues

Stumped? Maybe you can find a clue below.

-Glance
-Double-_____
-A work of nonfiction
-Prize
- Establishment of a pathogen after invasion
-Dinosaur adjective
-Relative _____
-_____ sheet
-Damp mist
-Smart person
-Organ _____

Arrange the circled letters to solve the mystery answer.

MYSTERY ANSWER ○○○○○○○○○○○○○○○○

PUZZLE 77

MEANS THE OPPOSITE

JUMBLE BrainBusters

Unscramble the Jumbles, one letter to each square, to spell pairs of words that have opposite or nearly opposite meanings.

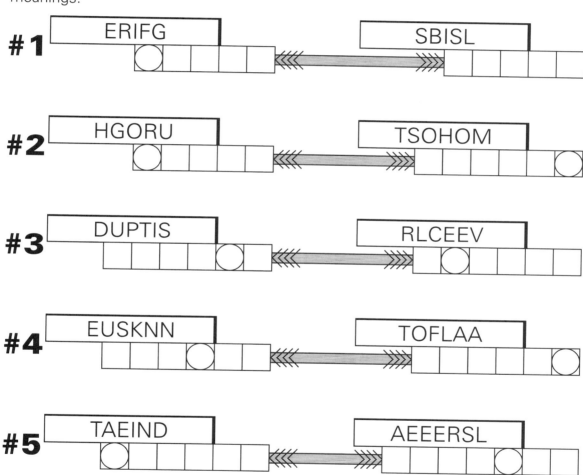

#1 ERIFG — SBISL

#2 HGORU — TSOHOM

#3 DUPTIS — RLCEEV

#4 EUSKNN — TOFLAA

#5 TAEIND — AEEERSL

Arrange the circled letters to solve the mystery answer. (Form two words that have the opposite or nearly opposite meanings.)

MYSTERY ANSWER ○○○○ — ○○○○○

TRIPLE JUMBLE® BRAINBUSTERS

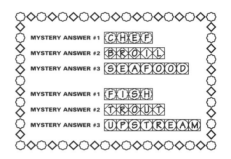

Unscramble the Jumbles, one letter to each square, to spell words.

#1 YTNTU

#2 FERVIY

#3 NGCAEH

#4 OPTRYH

#5 BGMEAL

#6 ALWPOL

MYSTERY ANSWER #1 CHEF
MYSTERY ANSWER #2 BROIL
MYSTERY ANSWER #3 SEAFOOD

MYSTERY ANSWER #1 FISH
MYSTERY ANSWER #2 TROUT
MYSTERY ANSWER #3 UPSTREAM

Box of Clues

Stumped? Maybe you can find a clue below. (No clues for the mystery answers.)

- Risk
- Check
- Trounce
- Award
- Switch
- Crazy

Arrange the clouded letters to solve mystery answer #1. Arrange the diamonded letters to solve mystery answer #2. Arrange the circled letters to solve mystery answer #3.
(The mystery answers will relate to each other.)

MYSTERY ANSWER #1

MYSTERY ANSWER #2

MYSTERY ANSWER #3

POETRY

JUMBLE BrainBusters

Unscramble the Jumbles, one letter to each square, to spell words found in the poem.

#1 TRIHG

#2 GOHTHTU

#3 NEDIRCLH

#4 ABHEEV

#5 NERERGE

Envy
by Kim E. Nolan

I envy the neighbors
That live ____ #1 next door
I ____ #2 I had nice things
But they have much more

Their ____ #3 ____ #4
And their car is brand new
The life that they have
I wish I had too

Although the adage seems simple
The lesson's quite hard
The grass always seems ____ #5
From in the next yard

Arrange the circled letters
to solve the mystery answer.
(The mystery answer is not
in the poem.)

MYSTERY ANSWER

MATH

Unscramble the Jumbled
letters, one letter to each square,
so that each equation is correct.

For example: NONTEOEOW
ONE + ONE = TWO

#1 TVFIEIEFNEV

☐☐☐☐◯ + ☐☐☐☐◯ = ☐◯☐

#2 GEEIHNEHOTIGT

☐◯☐☐☐ × ☐☐☐☐ = ☐☐☐☐◯☐

#3 FTOUWOUFROOTWR

◯☐☐ − ◯☐☐ = ☐☐☐◯☐ − ☐☐☐☐◯

#4 TVETELEEWOELWNV

☐☐☐☐☐☐☐ ÷ ☐☐☐☐☐☐◯ = ☐◯☐

#5 FNHEOEIEEEOTRVN

☐◯☐ + ☐☐◯☐ = ☐☐☐☐☐ − ☐◯☐☐☐

Then arrange the
circled letters to solve
the mystery equation. **MYSTERY EQUATION**

◯◯◯◯◯◯ × ◯◯◯◯◯◯ = ◯◯◯◯◯

JUMBLE JOKES

Unscramble the mixed up letters to reveal the punch lines as suggested by the jokes.

#1 What are strawberries when they are sad?

BERLEUERISB

#2 What's a rabbit's favorite game?

TSOCPHOCH

#3 What do you get if you put a snowman in a haunted house?

RCICEESMSA

#4 What do cats call their grandfather?

ARWGAPND

#5 What's very light, but can't be held for long?

AYUORETRHB

#6 How do you make a walnut laugh?

UCARITPKC

#7 What do you get from a dancing cow?

KIMKASESHL

ANIMALS

Unscramble the Jumbles, one letter to each square, to spell names of animals.

#1 LEGAE

#2 ALAML

#3 EACLM

#4 NOMYKE

#5 FIERFAG

#6 ASMUTKR

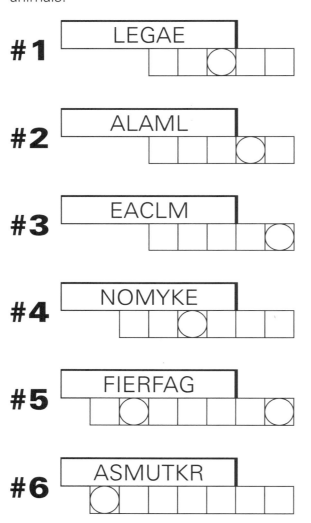

Box of Clues

Stumped? Maybe you can find a clue below.

-Spider _____
-A bird of prey
-South American camel relative
-Small, furry-footed rodent
-Desert mammal
-Tallest living quadruped
-A rodent with webbed hind feet

Arrange the circled letters to solve the mystery answer.

MYSTERY ANSWER

U.S. STATES

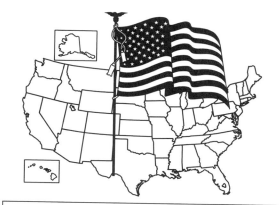

Unscramble the Jumbles, one letter to each square, to spell names of U.S. states.

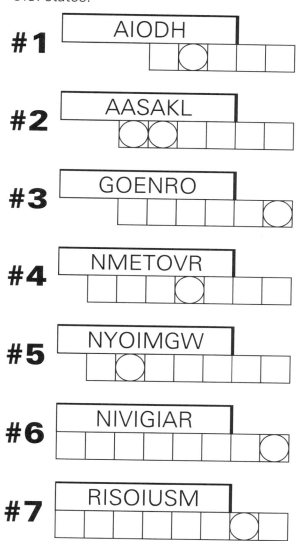

#1 AIODH

#2 AASAKL

#3 GOENRO

#4 NMETOVR

#5 NYOIMGW

#6 NIVIGIAR

#7 RISOIUSM

Box of Clues

Stumped? Maybe you can find a clue below.

- U.S. state that takes up more than 500,000 square miles
- Home to Salem
- U.S. state that leads the U.S. in lead production, based mainly in the Ozarks region
- Home to Cheyenne
- Home to the Potomac, Shenandoah, James, and Roanoke rivers
- Home to Burlington
- State originally inhabited by the Nanticoke and Piscataway Indian tribes
- Home to Boise

Arrange the circled letters to solve the mystery answer.

MYSTERY ANSWER

QUADRUPLE JUMBLE® BRAINBUSTERS

Unscramble the Jumbles, one letter to each square, to spell words.

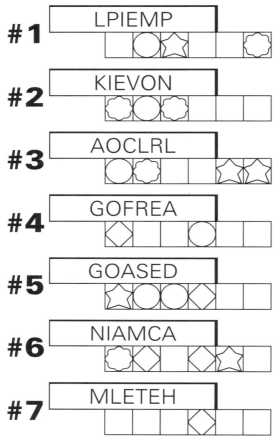

#1 LPIEMP

#2 KIEVON

#3 AOCLRL

#4 GOFREA

#5 GOASED

#6 NIAMCA

#7 MLETEH

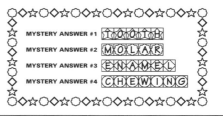

MYSTERY ANSWER #1 T O O T H
MYSTERY ANSWER #2 M O L A R
MYSTERY ANSWER #3 E N A M E L
MYSTERY ANSWER #4 C H E W I N G

Box of Clues

Stumped? Maybe you can find a clue below.
(No clues for the mystery answers.)

- To appeal to or cite as authority
- Inflamed elevation of the skin
- Lunatic
- Head protector
- Measured quantity of a therapeutic agent
- Dog _____
- Wander in search of food

Arrange the starred letters to solve mystery answer #1. Arrange the clouded letters to solve mystery answer #2. Arrange the diamonded letters to solve mystery answer #3. Arrange the circled letters to solve mystery answer #4.
(The mystery answers will relate to each other.)

MYSTERY ANSWER #1

MYSTERY ANSWER #2

MYSTERY ANSWER #3

MYSTERY ANSWER #4

AROUND THE HOME

JUMBLE BrainBusters

Unscramble the Jumbles, one letter to each square, to spell words related to the home.

#1 TOPIA

#2 NSIGID

#3 TSLECO

#4 DWOIWN

#5 TBHUBTA

#6 NOYLACB

#7 ARWEVDIY

Box of Clues

Stumped? Maybe you can find a clue below.

- Recreation area that adjoins a dwelling, often paved
- Bay _____
- Platform that projects from the wall of a building
- Path for vehicles
- Floor covering
- Bathing apparatus
- Broom _____
- Aluminum _____

Arrange the circled letters to solve the mystery answer.

MYSTERY ANSWER

ANIMALS

Unscramble the Jumbles, one letter to each square, to spell names of animals.

#1 RBCA

#2 WHKA

#3 AEGEL

#4 TLSHO

#5 OBONAB

#6 ENOYMK

#7 KRDARAAV

Arrange the circled letters to solve the mystery answer.

Box of Clues

Stumped? Maybe you can find a clue below.

-Golden _____
-Nonhuman primate mammal
-Ground _____
-Fish or pigeon _____
-Blue or hermit _____
-Large primate with a long, square, naked muzzle
-Rock _____
-Large, burrowing, nocturnal mammal

MYSTERY ANSWER

ABBREVIATIONS

Unscramble the Jumbles, one letter
to each square, to spell words that are
often abbreviated.

#1 CONEU

#2 UNAEEV

#3 NCEDSO

#4 EMNRBU

#5 AERWEYF

#6 DINULGIB

#7 TISCEADN

Arrange the circled letters
to solve the mystery answer.

MYSTERY ANSWER

ALL ABOUT ARIZONA

Unscramble the Jumbles, one letter to each square, to spell words related to Arizona.

#1 PIHO

#2 UAYM

#3 EROGG

#4 UACCST

#5 AVNJOA

#6 DAINISN

#7 EONHIXP

#8 FGFTASFAL

Arrange the circled letters to solve the mystery answer.

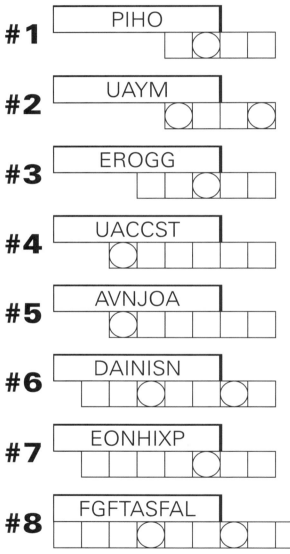

ARIZONA

Box of Clues

Stumped? Maybe you can find a clue below. (No clue for the mystery answer.)

- _____ National Monument
- Narrow, steep-walled canyon or part of a canyon
- City on the Colorado River
- American Indian people of northeastern Arizona
- Desert plant
- City on the Salt River
- Elevated Arizona city home to about 50,000
- Native Arizonans

MYSTERY ANSWER

PLAYING CARDS

Unscramble the Jumbles, one letter to each square, to spell words related to cards and card games.

#1 OFDL

#2 LIDW

#3 SLHUF

#4 UFLFB

#5 NTEITGB

#6 TGATISRH

Box of Clues

Stumped? Maybe you can find a clue below. (No clue for the mystery answer.)

-Starts with *B*; ends with *F*

-Starts with *B*; ends with *G*

-Starts with *F*; ends with *D*

-Starts with *W*; ends with *D*

-Starts with *F*; ends with *H*

-Starts with *S*; ends with *T*

Arrange the circled letters to solve the mystery answer.

MYSTERY ANSWER

COUNTRY FLAGS

Unscramble the Jumbles, one letter
to each square, to spell names of
countries, as suggested by the flags.

#1 PEYTG

#4 ARJOND

#2 SIRSAU

#5 EAIBLIR

#3 EKURYT

#6 MIGEUBL

Arrange the circled
letters to solve the
mystery answer.

MYSTERY ANSWER

RHYMING WORDS

JUMBLE
BrainBusters

Unscramble the Jumbles, one letter
to each square, to spell pairs of words
that rhyme.

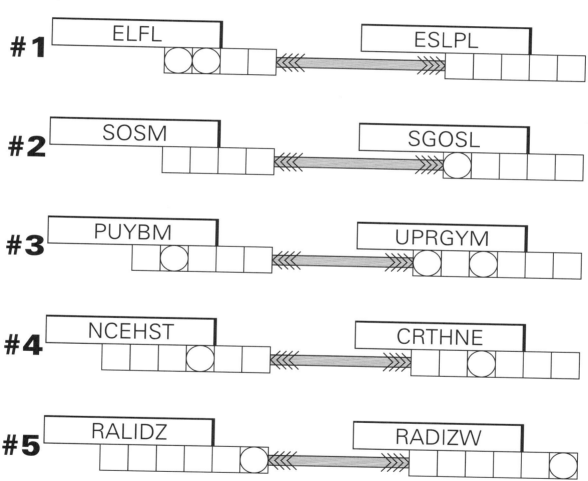

#1 ELFL ESLPL

#2 SOSM SGOSL

#3 PUYBM UPRGYM

#4 NCEHST CRTHNE

#5 RALIDZ RADIZW

Arrange the circled letters to solve the mystery answer.
(Form two words that rhyme.)

MYSTERY
ANSWER

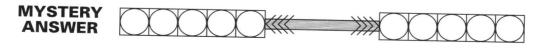

DOUBLE JUMBLE® BRAINBUSTERS

Unscramble the Jumbles, one letter to each square, to spell words.

#1 NTKIET

#2 TUIRSO

#3 ADIMLS

#4 RZADHA

#5 TOROPU

#6 EPMRCA

MYSTERY ANSWER #1 SUNNY
MYSTERY ANSWER #2 WEATHER

MYSTERY ANSWER #1 SPORTS
MYSTERY ANSWER #2 ATHLETES

MYSTERY ANSWER #1 COUNTRY
MYSTERY ANSWER #2 ETHIOPIA

Box of Clues

Stumped? Maybe you can find a clue below. (No clues for the mystery answers.)

-Dreadful
-Young feline
-One who courts a woman
-Remove as if by pulling up
-Portable dwelling
-Golf-course obstacle

Arrange the diamonded letters to solve mystery answer #1. Arrange the circled letters to solve mystery answer #2.
(The mystery answers will relate to each other.)

MYSTERY ANSWER #1

MYSTERY ANSWER #2

SEINFELD

JUMBLE BrainBusters

Unscramble the Jumbles, one letter to each square, to spell words related to the television show *Seinfeld*.

SEINFELD

#1 ANFKR

#2 DPYDU

#3 OCMOS

#4 AELEIN

#5 ERGOEG

#6 NWNAEM

#7 LIAMNMA

#8 BGNIHROE

Box of Clues

Stumped? Maybe you can find a clue below. (No clue for the mystery answer.)

-Elaine's boyfriend
-J.A. role
-Jerry's ex-girlfriend
-Kramer's first name
-George's father
-W.K. role
-C.K. to J.S.
-Newman, for example

Arrange the circled letters to solve the mystery answer.

MYSTERY ANSWER

WEATHER

JUMBLE BrainBusters

Unscramble the Jumbles, one letter to each square, to spell words related to weather.

#1 DIWNY

#2 LCICIE

#3 LYIHLC

#4 TALIEMC

#5 EGERSED

#6 GRHOUTD

#7 RZLIDAZB

Box of Clues

Stumped? Maybe you can find a clue below.

-Starts with *B*; ends with *D*
-Starts with *C*; ends with *Y*
-Starts with *W*; ends with *Y*
-Starts with *D*; ends with *S*
-Starts with *D*; ends with *T*
-Starts with *T*; ends with *R*
-Starts with *C*; ends with *E*
-Starts with *I*; ends with *E*

Arrange the circled letters to solve the mystery answer.

MYSTERY ANSWER

RHYMES WITH . . .

Unscramble the Jumbles, one letter to each square, to spell words that will each have a corresponding rhyming clue.

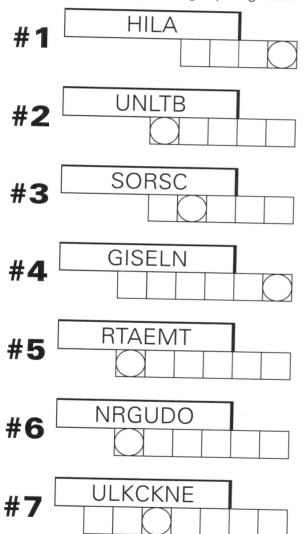

#1 HILA

#2 UNLTB

#3 SORSC

#4 GISELN

#5 RTAEMT

#6 NRGUDO

#7 ULKCKNE

TON - - - FUN
BACK - - - STACK
TRUCK - - - STUCK
MISTER - - - SISTER

Box of Clues

Stumped? Maybe you can find a clue below.

-Rhymes with *chuckle*
-Rhymes with *loss*
-Rhymes with *stunt*
-Rhymes with *found*
-Rhymes with *batter*
-Rhymes with *humble*
-Rhymes with *jingle*
-Rhymes with *rail*

Arrange the circled letters to solve the mystery answer.

MYSTERY ANSWER

JUMBLE JOKES

**JUMBLE.
BrainBusters**

Unscramble the mixed up letters to reveal the punch lines as suggested by the jokes.

#1 What do you get when you cross a giant with a skunk?

BAIGNTIKS

#2 What do you get from a pampered cow?

DPSILILOKEM

#3 What did the spider make on the computer?

TSABEIEW

#4 What can run but can't walk?

CAAUTFE

#5 What can be taken before you even get it?

ROYRUITUEPC

#6 What did the teddy bear say after it ate?

FTIMUAFEDS

#7 What bird is with you at every meal?

LAALWOSW

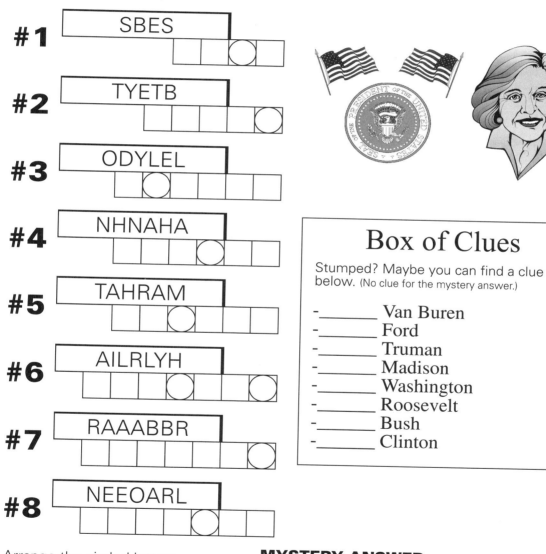

U.S. PRESIDENTIAL FIRST LADIES

JUMBLE.
BrainBusters

Unscramble the Jumbles, one letter to each square, to spell first names of U.S. presidential first ladies.

#1 SBES

#2 TYETB

#3 ODYLEL

#4 NHNAHA

#5 TAHRAM

#6 AILRLYH

#7 RAAABBR

#8 NEEOARL

Box of Clues

Stumped? Maybe you can find a clue below. (No clue for the mystery answer.)

- _____ Van Buren
- _____ Ford
- _____ Truman
- _____ Madison
- _____ Washington
- _____ Roosevelt
- _____ Bush
- _____ Clinton

Arrange the circled letters to solve the mystery answer.

MYSTERY ANSWER

ADJECTIVES

JUMBLE BrainBusters

Unscramble the Jumbles, one letter to each square, to spell adjectives.

#1 PIETN

#2 ZARYC

#3 NFIEIT

#4 CITATN

#5 TEIOCX

#6 HEALTL

#7 AGVURL

#8 TAITSND

Arrange the circled letters to solve the mystery answer.

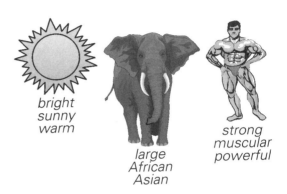

bright sunny warm

large African Asian

strong muscular powerful

Box of Clues

Stumped? Maybe you can find a clue below.

-Together
-Crude
-Adjacent
-Bumbling
-Deadly
-Screwy
-Aloof
-Limited
-Romantic, strange

MYSTERY ANSWER

CITY, COUNTRY

JUMBLE BrainBusters

Unscramble the Jumbles, one letter to each square, to spell names of cities and their corresponding countries.

For example:

CITY
NOORTOT
TORONTO,

COUNTRY
NCAAAD
CANADA

CITY

COUNTRIES

#1 ANAVHA , CBAU

#2 KYOOT , AANJP

#3 PIASR , CANEFR

#4 TAHSEN , RECEEG

#5 WOOSCM , SUSAIR

#6 DOONNL , GNNADEL

Arrange the circled letters to solve the mystery answers.

MYSTERY ANSWERS

CITY ◯◯◯◯◯◯ , COUNTRY ◯◯◯◯◯◯◯

PUZZLE 100

WARS AND THE MILITARY

JUMBLE BrainBusters

Unscramble the Jumbles, one letter to each square, to spell words related to wars and the military.

#1 LEUTBL

#2 TAYTER

#3 EGTRTA

#4 TFAIRARC

#5 YNIFRTNA

#6 KDALCEBO

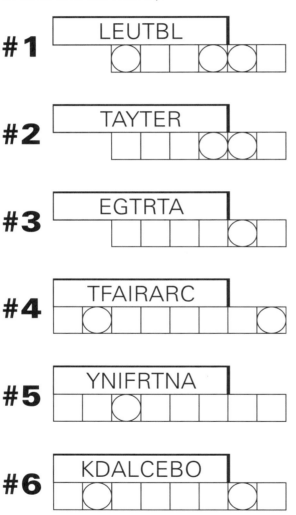

Box of Clues

Stumped? Maybe you can find a clue below.

- A fighter jet, for example
- Small missile
- Area of conflict
- Peace _____
- Soldiers trained, armed, and equipped to fight on foot
- Mark to shoot at
- Isolation by a warring nation of an enemy area (as a harbor) by troops

Arrange the circled letters to solve the mystery answer.

MYSTERY ANSWER

FASHION

JUMBLE
BrainBusters

Unscramble the Jumbles, one letter to each square, to spell words related to fashion and clothing.

#1 FTUITO

#2 EDUTOX

#3 RHSSTO

#4 EVLGSO

#5 FRUIOMN

#6 MNGRETA

#7 RWEETAS

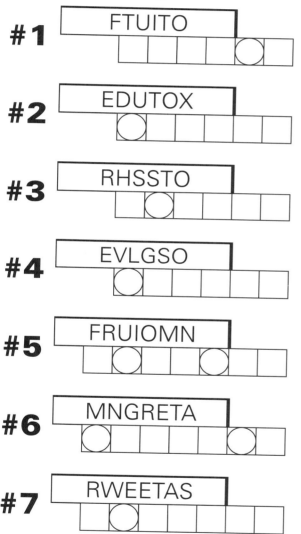

Interesting Fashion Facts

A pea jacket takes its name from the Dutch word *pij*, which is a sailor's garment.

Gold has been used as jewelry since about 4000 B.C.

Arrange the circled letters to solve the mystery answer.

MYSTERY ANSWER

COUNTRIES

Unscramble the Jumbles, one letter to each square, to spell names of countries.

#1 HLICE

#2 KYEUTR

#3 ROJNDA

#4 NOADLP

#5 AIBLIRE

#6 GRUHYAN

#7 MORIANA

Arrange the circled letters to solve the mystery answer.

Box of Clues

Stumped? Maybe you can find a clue below.

- Country with coastline on the Baltic Sea
- Slovakia's southern neighbor
- This country is divided roughly in half by the Tagus River
- Country that shares its name with the last name of a famous basketball player
- Cold-sounding country
- The Danube River forms the southern boundary of this European country
- African country on the Atlantic
- Country that shares its name with a bird

MYSTERY ANSWER

MAKING MOVIES

Unscramble the Jumbles, one letter to each square, to spell words related to making movies.

#1 FMIL

#2 HAIRC

#3 OPRPS

#4 TCSRIP

#5 AETERK

#6 KAEPMU

#7 CTEFESF

Box of Clues

Stumped? Maybe you can find a clue below.

-Subsequent filming
-Supporting objects
-Special _____
-Practice
-Radiation-sensitive tape
-Actors' cosmetics
-Director's seat
-Written directions

Arrange the circled letters to solve the mystery answer.

MYSTERY ANSWER

PUZZLE 104

DRAWING / PAINTING

Unscramble the Jumbles, one letter to each square, to spell words related to drawing and painting.

#1 AEPRP

#2 NELCIP

#3 CTSEHK

#4 NCAAVS

#5 SEARRE

#6 RCANOY

Arrange the circled letters to solve the mystery answer.

Box of Clues

Stumped? Maybe you can find a clue below.

- Painters fabric
- Graph _____
- Colorful writing instrument
- Slender writing instrument
- This is used to fix a mistake
- Organized instruction
- An aimless or casual scribble, design, or sketch

MYSTERY ANSWER

STATE CAPITALS

JUMBLE. BrainBusters

Unscramble the Jumbles, one letter to each square, to names of U.S. state capitals.

#1 SOIBE

#2 KOETAP

#3 NNCOILL

#4 PINEOXH

#5 MOYIAPL

#6 NORETNT

#7 HICORDMN

Box of Clues

Stumped? Maybe you can find a clue below. (No clue for the mystery answer.)

-Starts with *O*; ends with *A*
-Starts with *T*; ends with *A*
-Starts with *P*; ends with *X*
-Starts with *R*; ends with *D*
-Starts with *T*; ends with *N*
-Starts with *L*; ends with *N*
-Starts with *B*; ends with *E*

Arrange the circled letters to solve the mystery answer.

MYSTERY ANSWER

STARTS WITH *L*

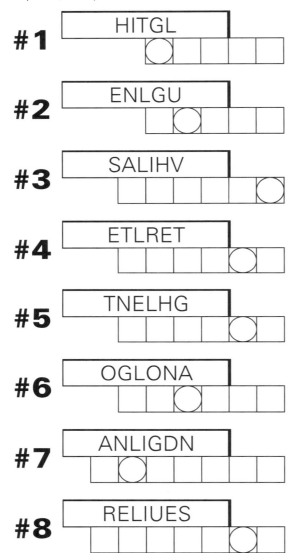

JUMBLE BrainBusters

Unscramble the Jumbles, one letter to each square, to spell words that start with *L*.

#1 HITGL

#2 ENLGU

#3 SALIHV

#4 ETLRET

#5 TNELHG

#6 OGLONA

#7 ANLIGDN

#8 RELIUES

Arrange the circled letters to solve the mystery answer.

Box of Clues

Stumped? Maybe you can find a clue below.

- _____ suit
- Shallow body of water
- Moon _____
- Extravagant
- Duration
- Green _____
- Amused sound
- Greek _____
- Sudden forward rush or reach

MYSTERY ANSWER

SPORTS

JUMBLE
BrainBusters

Unscramble the Jumbles, one letter to each square, to spell words related to sports.

#1 OEROIK

#2 BLFEMU

#3 LTOAFLBS

#4 DLCSEEUH

#5 NIMSIWGM

#6 SNTNIASDG

Box of Clues

Stumped? Maybe you can find a clue below. (No clue for the mystery answer.)

-Sport invented in Chicago
-Novice
-A football mistake
-Compilation of all team records and rankings
-Calendar of games
-Spitz's Olympic sport

Arrange the circled letters to solve the mystery answer.

MYSTERY ANSWER

SUPER JUMBLE CHALLENGE

JUMBLE BrainBusters

#1 CAE

Unscramble the Jumbles, one letter to each square, to spell words.

#2 OKOB

#3 DRIOA

#4 ANGMEA

#5 OLAONLB

#6 NDACIETC

#7 ATILINONF

#8 SUONTERDOD

#9 EIMRENTVPMO

#10 BURNASOEALEN

Box of Clues

Stumped? Maybe you can find a clue below.

-Weather _____
-A result of a great serve
-Unqualified, absolute
-Rise in general price levels
-Absurd, invalid, irrational
-_____ frequency
-Enhancement
-Grasped
-Novel
-_____-prone
-Get by

Arrange the circled letters to solve the mystery answer.

MYSTERY ANSWER

CHEERS

JUMBLE® BrainBusters

Unscramble the Jumbles, one letter to each square, to spell words related to the television show *Cheers*.

#1 ELYAL

#2 ACCHO

#3 DWOYO

#4 NADNOS

#5 SOBOTN

#6 SRERFIA

#7 TPCIRHE

#8 ELHLYSE

#9 STAIRSEW

Box of Clues

Stumped? Maybe you can find a clue below. (No clue for the mystery answer.)

-K.G. role
-Actress' first name who played D.C.
-1987 *Cheers* addition
-N.C. role
-Tavern's surroundings
-1985 *Cheers* addition
-Leading man
-Sam's sporting position
-Carla, for example

Arrange the circled letters to solve the mystery answer.

MYSTERY ANSWER

STARTS WITH AND ENDS WITH A VOWEL

Unscramble the Jumbles, one letter to each square, to spell words that start with and end with a vowel.

#1 CEOH

#2 DIAOH

#3 GOEAM

#4 CAIEVD

#5 LAAEZB

#6 KEIOMS

#7 RIUSATA

Arrange the circled letters to solve the mystery answer.

Box of Clues

Stumped? Maybe you can find a clue below.

- The 24th and last of its kind
- On fire
- One of fifty
- Good or bad _____
- A tropical fruit
- Extreme northerner
- European country
- Repetition of a sound

MYSTERY ANSWER

MOVIES

JUMBLE BrainBusters

Unscramble the Jumbles, one letter to each square, to spell names of movies.

#1 KROYC

#2 TACCOTN

#3 NFTSAIAA

#4 RIHOSESO

#5 HANWIONTC

#6 DTSHEIERIN

#7 RVTXIRIEDA

Box of Clues

Stumped? Maybe you can find a clue below.

- 1986 G.H. movie about a coach
- 1976 S.S. movie
- 1973 horror movie
- 1997 J.F. movie
- 1976 R.D. movie directed by Martin Scorsese
- 1940 animated Disney musical
- 1999 movie based on a true story
- 1974 J.N. movie

Arrange the circled letters to solve the mystery answer.

MYSTERY ANSWER

MATH

Unscramble the Jumbled
letters, one letter to each square,
so that each equation is correct.

For example: NOLSOEPNEU
ONE PLUS ONE = TWO

#1 NETELFIPFIUVVES

☐☐◯☐ ☐◯☐☐☐ ☐☐☐◯ = ☐☐◯

#2 NMOEIUSONEERONZ

☐☐◯☐ ☐☐◯☐☐ ☐☐☐☐ = ☐◯☐☐

#3 UNSIPLTSREIEEHNX

☐☐◯ ◯◯☐☐ ☐☐☐◯ = ☐◯☐☐

#4 SSVNEIMUFIETNOVEW

◯☐☐☐☐ ☐☐☐☐☐ ☐☐◯ = ☐☐☐

#5 FTOMTIEOHUSREITWG

☐☐☐☐ ☐◯☐◯ ◯☐☐☐ = ☐☐☐☐☐

Then arrange the
circled letters to solve
the mystery equation. **MYSTERY EQUATION**

◯◯◯ ◯◯◯◯ ◯◯◯◯ = ◯◯◯◯◯◯

PHOTOGRAPHY

Unscramble the Jumbles, one letter
to each square, to spell words related
to photography.

#1 GTLIH

#2 AFLHS

#3 COSUF

#4 ROLOC

#5 RYBRUL

#6 SRCOTATN

#7 REOXUESP

Arrange the circled letters
to solve the mystery answer.

Box of Clues

Stumped? Maybe you can find a clue
below.

-Artificial light source
-Out of focus
-Degree of difference between
 the lightest and darkest parts
 of a picture
-At least some is needed in
 order to take a normal photo
-Make clear
-_____ speed
-The intensity of light falling on
 a photographic film or plate
-_____ film

MYSTERY ANSWER

MYSTERY PERSON

JUMBLE BrainBusters

Unscramble the Jumbles, one letter to each square, to spell words that relate to the mystery person.

#1 OIOH

#2 AGRNMO

#3 TPETSNA

#4 NIEOVRNT

#5 SEDAESFN

#6 ERNEEWYJS

#7 ROLAOABRYT

Box of Clues

Use the clues below to help you solve the seven Jumbles.

- This person was strongly motivated by efforts to overcome his handicap of partial _____
- He was born in Milan, _____
- His profession
- He created the world's first industrial-research laboratory in this U.S. state
- He was advanced $30,000 by such financiers as J. P. _____ and the Vanderbilts
- His workplace
- He holds a record number of these

Arrange the circled letters to solve the mystery person.

MYSTERY PERSON

MATH

JUMBLE BrainBusters

Unscramble the Jumbled
letters, one letter to each square,
so that each equation is correct.

For example: NONTEOEOW
ONE + ONE = TWO

#1 LNEIFIEEXVESV

◯ ☐ ☐ + ☐ ◯ ☐ = ☐ ☐ ◯ ☐ ☐ ☐

#2 RIGHFTNYOTUTEYEW

☐ ◯ ☐ ☐ ÷ ☐ ☐ ☐ ☐ = ☐ ☐ ☐ ☐ ◯ ☐

#3 TNTRTEZNTNEOEWEY

☐ ☐ ◯ + ☐ ☐ ☐ = ☐ ◯ ☐ ☐ ☐ + ☐ ◯ ☐ ☐

#4 RITSTTYITIYHYTXRH

☐ ◯ ☐ ☐ ◯ ☐ + ☐ ☐ ◯ ☐ ☐ = ☐ ☐ ◯ ☐ ☐

#5 FWOVTOOUTELEURWFR

☐ ☐ ☐ × ☐ ☐ ☐ ☐ = ◯ ☐ ☐ ☐ ◯ − ☐ ◯ ☐ ☐

Then arrange the
circled letters to solve
the mystery equation.

MYSTERY EQUATION

◯◯◯◯◯◯ × ◯◯◯ = ◯◯◯◯◯◯◯◯

117

MEANS THE SAME

JUMBLE BrainBusters

Unscramble the Jumbles, one letter to each square, to spell pairs of words that have the same or similar meanings.

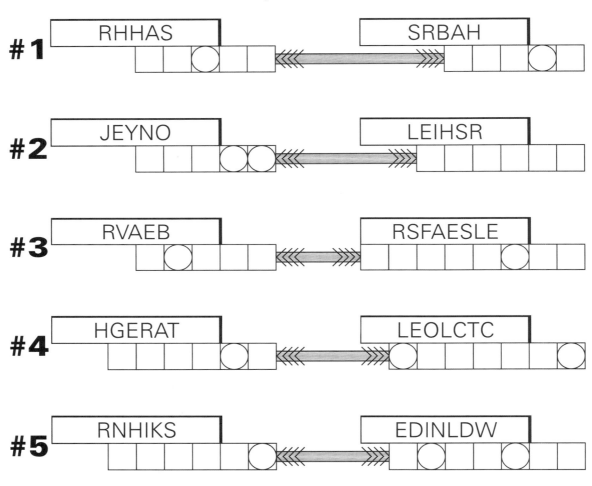

#1 RHHAS — SRBAH

#2 JEYNO — LEIHSR

#3 RVAEB — RSFAESLE

#4 HGERAT — LEOLCTC

#5 RNHIKS — EDINLDW

Arrange the circled letters to solve the mystery answer.
(Form two words that have the same or similar meanings.)

MYSTERY ANSWER

TRIPLE JUMBLE® BRAINBUSTERS

Unscramble the Jumbles, one letter to each square, to spell words.

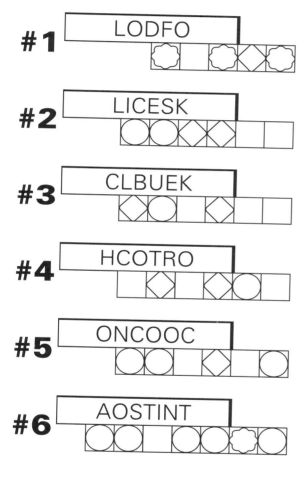

#1 LODFO

#2 LICESK

#3 CLBUEK

#4 HCOTRO

#5 ONCOOC

#6 AOSTINT

MYSTERY ANSWER #1

MYSTERY ANSWER #2

MYSTERY ANSWER #3

JUMBLE BrainBusters

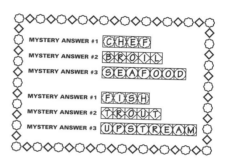

MYSTERY ANSWER #1 CHEF
MYSTERY ANSWER #2 BROIL
MYSTERY ANSWER #3 SEAFOOD

MYSTERY ANSWER #1 FISH
MYSTERY ANSWER #2 TROUT
MYSTERY ANSWER #3 UPSTREAM

Box of Clues

Stumped? Maybe you can find a clue below. (No clues for the mystery answers.)

- Silky envelope
- Result of too much rain
- Belt _____
- Agricultural implement
- Channel
- Associate

Arrange the clouded letters to solve mystery answer #1. Arrange the diamonded letters to solve mystery answer #2. Arrange the circled letters to solve mystery answer #3.
(The mystery answers will relate to each other.)

OCCUPATIONS

Unscramble the Jumbles, one letter
to each square, to spell names of
occupations.

#1 NABEKR

#2 TUAROH

#3 EAIRWT

#4 ESCIRHA

#5 OESRNGU

#6 CAUSINIM

Arrange the circled letters
to solve the mystery answer.

Box of Clues

Stumped? Maybe you can find a clue
below.

-Starts with *C*; ends with *R*
-Starts with *M*; ends with *N*
-Starts with *W*; ends with *R*
-Starts with *M*; ends with *C*
-Starts with *S*; ends with *N*
-Starts with *A*; ends with *R*
-Starts with *B*; ends with *R*

MYSTERY ANSWER

HEALTH

Unscramble the Jumbles, one letter to each square, to spell words related to human health.

#1 APISNR

#2 OTDRCO

#3 TGWIHE

#4 RAINSIP

#5 ETFIGAU

#6 TAPOILHS

#7 EUTRARFC

Arrange the circled letters to solve the mystery answer.

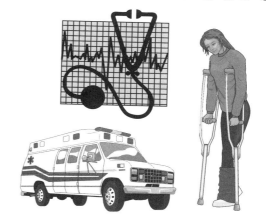

JUMBLE BrainBusters

Box of Clues

Stumped? Maybe you can find a clue below.

- _____ room or bed
- Break
- "Watched" total
- Sudden twist or wrench of a joint with stretching or tearing of ligaments
- Surgeon
- White crystalline derivative $C_9H_8O_4$ of salicylic acid
- Painful condition and a reason to take aspirin
- Weariness

MYSTERY ANSWER

QUADRUPLE JUMBLE® BRAINBUSTERS

Unscramble the Jumbles, one letter to each square, to spell words.

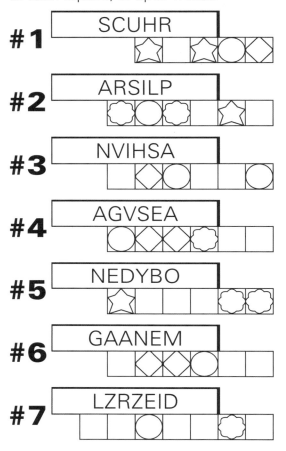

#1 SCUHR

#2 ARSILP

#3 NVIHSA

#4 AGVSEA

#5 NEDYBO

#6 GAANEM

#7 LZRZEID

JUMBLE BrainBusters

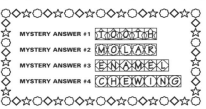

MYSTERY ANSWER #1 [D][O][C][T][O][R]
MYSTERY ANSWER #2 [M][O][L][A][R]
MYSTERY ANSWER #3 [E][N][A][M][E][L]
MYSTERY ANSWER #4 [C][H][E][W][I][N][G]

Box of Clues

Stumped? Maybe you can find a clue below.
(No clues for the mystery answers.)

-Get by
-Path of a point in a plane moving around a central point while continuously receding from or approaching it
-Light rain
-Beat by a large margin
-Primitive person
-Farther or in addition
-Disappear

Arrange the starred letters to solve mystery answer #1. Arrange the clouded letters to solve mystery answer #2. Arrange the diamonded letters to solve mystery answer #3. Arrange the circled letters to solve mystery answer #4.
(The mystery answers will relate to each other.)

MYSTERY ANSWER #1

MYSTERY ANSWER #2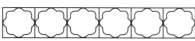

MYSTERY ANSWER #3

MYSTERY ANSWER #4

ALL ABOUT MUSIC

JUMBLE. BrainBusters

Unscramble the Jumbles, one letter to each square, to spell words related to music.

#1 POERA

#2 NIOILV

#3 RAMOTZ

#4 EGALROL

#5 RCTOCEN

#6 RSMUEAE

#7 NOYAMHR

Box of Clues

Stumped? Maybe you can find a clue below.

-At a brisk, lively tempo
-Drama set to music
-Performance
-Pleasant combination of simultaneous sounds
-Orchestral concert piece written especially as a single movement in sonata form
-Stringed instrument
-Famous composer
-Grouping of a specified number of musical beats

Arrange the circled letters to solve the mystery answer.

MYSTERY ANSWER

STARTS WITH N

JUMBLE.
BrainBusters

Unscramble the Jumbles, one letter to each square, to spell words that start with N.

#1 NONU

#2 OLVNE

#3 GNUED

#4 ANIVET

#5 ENELED

#6 BNILEM

#7 AONRWR

#8 NTNOIHG

Arrange the circled letters to solve the mystery answer.

Box of Clues

Stumped? Maybe you can find a clue below.

-Book
-Word classification
-_____ American
-Zip, zero
-Prod lightly
-George Jefferson to Archie Bunker in the beginning
-Agile
-Pine _____
-Skinny, little

MYSTERY ANSWER

ALL ABOUT TRAINS

Unscramble the Jumbles, one letter to each square, to spell words related to trains.

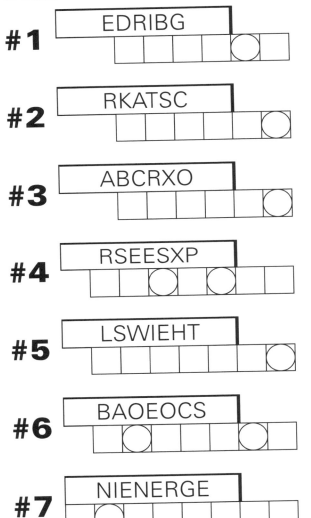

#1 EDRIBG

#2 RKATSC

#3 ABCRXO

#4 RSEESXP

#5 LSWIEHT

#6 BAOEOCS

#7 NIENERGE

Box of Clues

Stumped? Maybe you can find a clue below.

- This has sliding doors and is used to haul freight
- Rider
- Pair of parallel rails
- Train with very few stops
- Supervisor
- Train sounding device
- Last car
- One way to get a train across water or a major road

Arrange the circled letters to solve the mystery answer.

MYSTERY ANSWER

U.S. PRESIDENTS

JUMBLE
BrainBusters

Unscramble the Jumbles,
one letter to each square,
to spell the first and last
names of U.S. presidents.

#1 HOLEJRTNY

#2 MJSOELKAP

#3 HADSJNOMA

#4 FEORLDRDGA

#5 EREHEROTORHVB

#6 TCEAERHRUTRSH

#7 DAREONAKSJNWC

Arrange the circled
letters to solve the
mystery answer.

MYSTERY ANSWER

HAPPY DAYS

Unscramble the Jumbles, one letter to each square, to spell words related to the television show *Happy Days*.

#1 SROS

#2 CIEIHR

#3 ZFIENO

#4 NIOJEA

#5 SOCINU

#6 HOETMR

#7 RAHDWO

#8 ARMGIARE

#9 DWARRHAE

Box of Clues

Stumped? Maybe you can find a clue below. (No clue for the mystery answer.)

-E.M. role
-Richie and Lori Beth's ceremony
-Howard's store type
-Marion _____
-R.H. role
-Chachi to Fonzie
-T.B. role
-H.W. role
-M.C. to R.C. and J.C.

Arrange the circled letters to solve the mystery answer.

MYSTERY ANSWER

ANIMALS

JUMBLE BrainBusters

Unscramble the Jumbles, one letter to each square, to spell names of animals.

#1 SBINO

#2 DAAPN

#3 MUERL

#4 ACRONOC

#5 NHEEATLP

#6 LRADIMLN

#7 KCIMNUHP

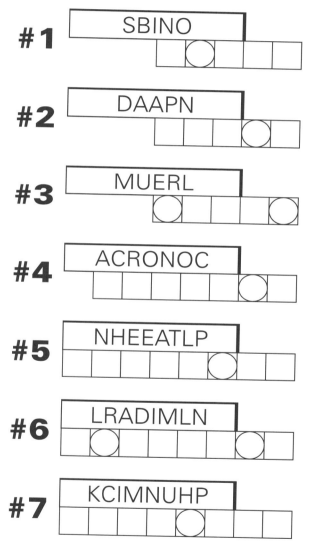

Box of Clues

Stumped? Maybe you can find a clue below.

- Starts with *P*; ends with *A*
- Starts with *R*; ends with *N*
- Starts with *M*; ends with *L*
- Starts with *C*; ends with *K*
- Starts with *A*; ends with *O*
- Starts with *L*; ends with *R*
- Starts with *B*; ends with *N*
- Starts with *E*; ends with *T*

Arrange the circled letters to solve the mystery answer.

MYSTERY ANSWER

ALL ABOUT MONEY

Unscramble the Jumbles, one letter to each square, to spell words related to money.

#1 AUVEL

#2 EANBRK

#3 RSAYAL

#4 CINEOM

#5 LEATLW

#6 VEEUENR

#7 TSIEETRN

#8 DLILOFBL

Box of Clues

Stumped? Maybe you can find a clue below. (No clue for the mystery answer.)

-Transportable money holder
-_____ tax
-Fixed compensation
-Worth
-Lending institution professional
-_____ rate
-Used to transport paper money
-Internal _____ Service

Arrange the circled letters to solve the mystery answer.

MYSTERY ANSWER

DOUBLE JUMBLE® BRAINBUSTERS

Unscramble the Jumbles, one letter to each square, to spell words.

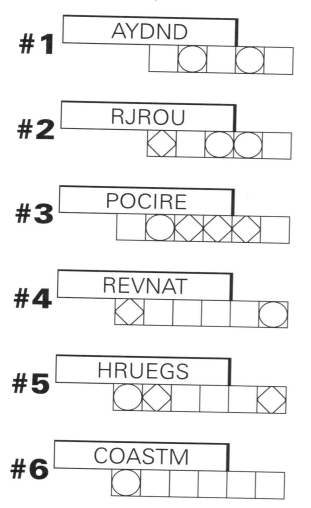

#1 AYDND

#2 RJROU

#3 POCIRE

#4 REVNAT

#5 HRUEGS

#6 COASTM

JUMBLE BrainBusters

MYSTERY ANSWER #1 SUNNY
MYSTERY ANSWER #2 WEATHER

MYSTERY ANSWER #1 SPORTS
MYSTERY ANSWER #2 ATHLETES

MYSTERY ANSWER #1 COUNTRY
MYSTERY ANSWER #2 ETHIOPIA

Box of Clues

Stumped? Maybe you can find a clue below. (No clues for the mystery answers.)

-Oil well with a copious natural flow
-Duplicator
-Symbolic figure
-Courtroom decision maker
-Bar
-Fine's partner

Arrange the diamonded letters to solve mystery answer #1. Arrange the circled letters to solve mystery answer #2.
(The mystery answers will relate to each other.)

MYSTERY ANSWER #1

MYSTERY ANSWER #2

PUZZLE 129

ALL ABOUT CHESS

JUMBLE BrainBusters

Unscramble the Jumbles, one letter to each square, to spell words related to chess.

#1 OROK

#2 ANPW

#3 VEMO

#4 CIPEE

#5 GHNITK

#6 SIOPBH

#7 RAEPUTC

#8 NESFEED

Arrange the circled letters to solve the mystery answer.

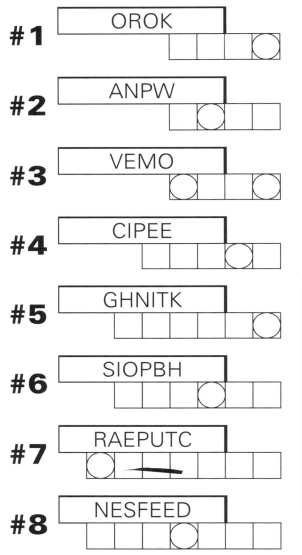

Chess Q & A

QUESTION:
How many ways are there to play the first 10 moves in a game of chess?

ANSWER:
169,518,829,100,544,000

MYSTERY ANSWER

POETRY

Unscramble the Jumbles, one letter to each square, to spell words found in the poem.

#1 HGSIT

#2 ULODHS

#3 GREEM

#4 NGURNIN

#5 NPORDE

#6 RTCIANE

Traffic

by Kim E. Nolan

Bumper to bumper
With no end in ____ #1
____ #2 I stay in my lane?
Can I ____ #3 left or right?

I'm ____ #4 quite late
The miles inch past
This confounded construction
How long will it last?

It feels like an eternity
As I near my destination
I ____ #5 my return trip
And ____ #6 aggravation

Arrange the circled letters
to solve the mystery answer.
(The mystery answer is not
in the poem.)

MYSTERY ANSWER

ENDS IN *I*

Unscramble the Jumbles, one letter to each square, to spell words that end in *I*.

JUMBLE BrainBusters

MIAMI   SAFARI
GANDHI   BIKINI

Ends in

GEMINI   TAHITI   ALKALI
SCAMPI   HAITI

#1 GIYO

#2 IKIBIN

#3 FIASAR

#4 MAAILS

#5 ARIOLIV

#6 CIHAHIB

#7 CUINIHCZ

Arrange the circled letters to solve the mystery answer.

Box of Clues

Stumped? Maybe you can find a clue below. (No clue for the mystery answer.)

-Expedition
-Highly seasoned sausage of pork and beef either dried or fresh
-Charcoal brazier
-Summer squash of bushy growth with smooth, cylindrical, usually dark green fruit
-Revealing garment
-Type of filled pasta
-Markedly reflective or mystical person

MYSTERY ANSWER

TRIPLE JUMBLE BRAINBUSTERS

Unscramble the Jumbles, one letter to each square, to spell words.

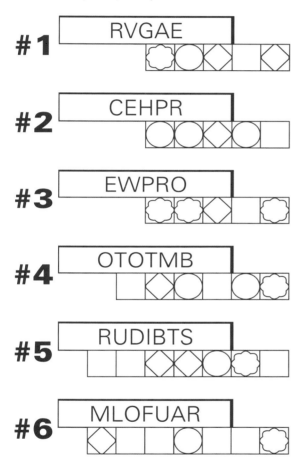

#1 RVGAE

#2 CEHPR

#3 EWPRO

#4 OTOTMB

#5 RUDIBTS

#6 MLOFUAR

JUMBLE BrainBusters

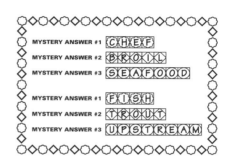

MYSTERY ANSWER #1 CHEF
MYSTERY ANSWER #2 BROIL
MYSTERY ANSWER #3 SEAFOOD

MYSTERY ANSWER #1 FISH
MYSTERY ANSWER #2 TROUT
MYSTERY ANSWER #3 UPSTREAM

Box of Clues

Stumped? Maybe you can find a clue below. (No clues for the mystery answers.)

- Recipe, prescription
- Base
- Serious, somber
- Roost for a bird
- Force, energy
- Bother

Arrange the clouded letters to solve mystery answer #1. Arrange the diamonded letters to solve mystery answer #2. Arrange the circled letters to solve mystery answer #3.
(The mystery answers will relate to each other.)

MYSTERY ANSWER #1

MYSTERY ANSWER #2

MYSTERY ANSWER #3

COMPUTERS

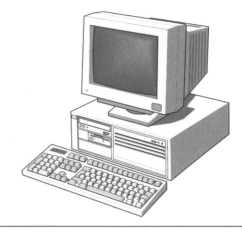

Unscramble the Jumbles, one letter to each square, to spell words related to computers.

#1 AATD

#2 LCIKC

#3 SEUMO

#4 TEELED

#5 YMMREO

#6 NEPIMTU

#7 MGAORPR

#8 ROEBAYDK

Box of Clues

Stumped? Maybe you can find a clue below.

- This is used to operate a computer
- Curser controller
- Double-_____
- An Intel trademark
- Information
- Harvard dropout
- Sequence of coded instructions that can be inserted into a mechanism
- Virtual _____
- Remove

Arrange the circled letters to solve the mystery answer.

MYSTERY ANSWER

SUPER JUMBLE® CHALLENGE

JUMBLE BrainBusters

Unscramble the Jumbles, one letter to each square, to spell words.

#1 PPO

#2 WLKA

#3 MLAPC

#4 CESPEA

#5 TOOIRMN

#6 AEHICPWT

#7 TNATRIYME

#8 ATAILITFCE

#9 AXMAROITEPP

#10 ERDMIANUESVT

Box of Clues

Stumped? Maybe you can find a clue below.

-Reckon
-Wave crest
-Constricting device
-Calamity
-Soda nickname
-Amazing, stupendous
-Help bring about
-_____ velocity
-_____ leave
-Base on balls
-Screen

Arrange the circled letters to solve the mystery answer.

MYSTERY ANSWER

137

GOING TO THE DENTIST

Unscramble the Jumbles, one letter to each square, to spell words related to going to the dentist.

#1 CAEYD

#2 NWROC

#3 ERCSAB

#4 UQLAEP

#5 LMEENA

#6 NIFIGLL

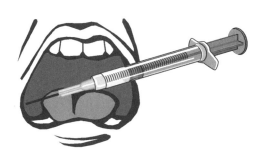

Box of Clues

Stumped? Maybe you can find a clue below. (No clue for the mystery answer.)

-Tooth _____
-Cavity fix
-Hard calcareous substance
-A film of mucus that harbors bacteria
-Dental appliances
-Part of a tooth external to the gum or an artificial substitute for this

Arrange the circled letters to solve the mystery answer.

MYSTERY ANSWER

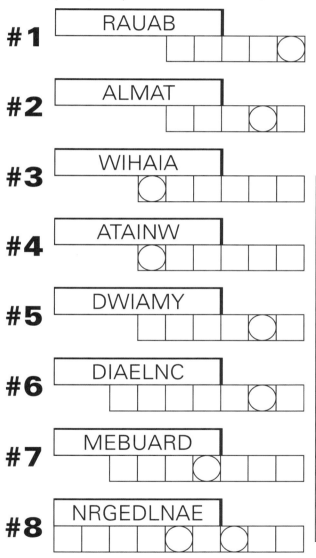

ISLANDS

Unscramble the Jumbles, one letter to each square, to spell names of Islands.

#1 RAUAB

#2 ALMAT

#3 WIHAIA

#4 ATAINW

#5 DWIAMY

#6 DIAELNC

#7 MEBUARD

#8 NRGEDLNAE

Arrange the circled letters to solve the mystery answer.

Box of Clues

Stumped? Maybe you can find a clue below.

- Island off the coast of China
- The "Big Island"
- Island south of Sicily in the Mediterranean Sea
- Island in the north Atlantic
- Island in the Lesser Antilles off the coast of Venezuela
- World's largest island
- Island in the Atlantic, home to Hamilton
- Metropolitan island home to millions
- Unincorporated U.S. territory in the Pacific where a famous World War II battle was fought

MYSTERY ANSWER

"COLORFUL" WORDS

Unscramble the Jumbles, one letter to each square, to spell words that have a color in their name, as shown in the examples.

JUMBLE BrainBusters

For example:

REDUCE

BLUEBIRD

BLACKBIRD

WHITEWALL

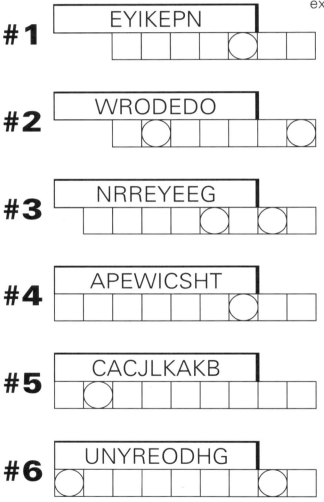

#1 EYIKEPN

#2 WRODEDO

#3 NRREYEEG

#4 APEWICSHT

#5 CACJLKAKB

#6 UNYREODHG

Box of Clues

Stumped? Maybe you can find a clue below. (No clue for the mystery answer.)

-Foliage or plants
-Type of game
-Fast canine
-Breaking waves
-Large tree
-Highly contagious conjunctivitis

Arrange the circled letters to solve the mystery answer.

MYSTERY ANSWER

MATH

JUMBLE BrainBusters

Unscramble the Jumbled letters, one letter to each square, so that each equation is correct.

For example: NONTEOEOW
ONE + ONE = TWO

#1 ZETNENEORT

☐◯☐ − ◯☐☐ = ☐☐◯☐

#2 FENVOIEIEFV

☐☐☐◯ ÷ ☐☐◯☐ = ◯☐☐☐

#3 WRFETTYNOU

◯☐◯◯◯ × FIVE = ☐◯☐☐◯☐

#4 XSISEIFVXEVESIN

☐☐☐☐ + ☐☐☐☐ = ☐☐☐◯ + ☐☐☐◯

#5 TLWEVNOHIEEERNTET

☐◯☐☐☐☐ + ☐☐☐☐ = ☐◯☐☐☐☐☐☐

Then arrange the circled letters to solve the mystery equation.

MYSTERY EQUATION

◯◯◯◯◯◯ ÷ ◯◯◯◯ = ◯◯◯◯◯

141

QUADRUPLE JUMBLE® BRAINBUSTERS

Unscramble the Jumbles, one letter to each square, to spell words.

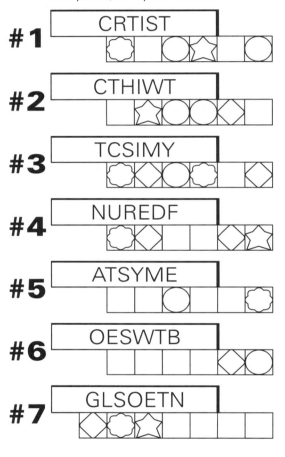

#1 CRTIST

#2 CTHIWT

#3 TCSIMY

#4 NUREDF

#5 ATSYME

#6 OESWTB

#7 GLSOETN

MYSTERY ANSWER #1

MYSTERY ANSWER #2

MYSTERY ANSWER #3

MYSTERY ANSWER #4

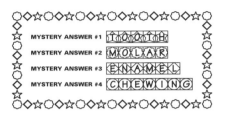

MYSTERY ANSWER #1 TOOTH
MYSTERY ANSWER #2 MOLAR
MYSTERY ANSWER #3 ENAMEL
MYSTERY ANSWER #4 CHEWING

Box of Clues

Stumped? Maybe you can find a clue below.
(No clues for the mystery answers.)

-Mysterious, enigmatic
-Stringent
-Return money in restitution
-Hot and humid
-Give
-Lengthiest
-Move or pull with a sudden motion

Arrange the starred letters to solve mystery answer #1. Arrange the clouded letters to solve mystery answer #2. Arrange the diamonded letters to solve mystery answer #3. Arrange the circled letters to solve mystery answer #4.
(The mystery answers will relate to each other.)

ANIMAL GROUPINGS

JUMBLE BrainBusters

Unscramble the Jumbles, one letter to each square, to spell names of animals.

#1 ELUSM

#2 TBRAISB

#3 REEASVB

#4 FAUOFLB

#5 NKHIECSC

#6 EFIASRGF

#7 AIROLSGL

Arrange the circled letters to solve the mystery answer.

Box of Clues

Stumped? Maybe you can find a clue below.

#1) A group of these is called a barren or pack

#2) A group of these is called a colony

#3) A group of these is called a colony

#4) A group of these is called a herd, gang, or obstinacy

#5) A group of these is called a brood or clutch

#6) A group of these is called a herd or tower

#7) A group of these is called a band

M.A.) A group of these is called a stand

MYSTERY ANSWER

DOUBLE JUMBLE® BRAINBUSTERS

Unscramble the Jumbles, one letter to each square, to spell words.

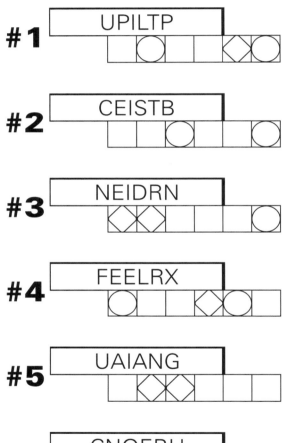

#1 UPILTP

#2 CEISTB

#3 NEIDRN

#4 FEELRX

#5 UAIANG

#6 CNOEBU

MYSTERY ANSWER #1 SUNNY
MYSTERY ANSWER #2 WEATHER

MYSTERY ANSWER #1 SPORTS
MYSTERY ANSWER #2 ATHLETES

MYSTERY ANSWER #1 COUNTRY
MYSTERY ANSWER #2 ETHIOPIA

Box of Clues

Stumped? Maybe you can find a clue below. (No clues for the mystery answers.)

-Inborn response
-Cut down the middle
-Rebound
-_____ table
-Type of lizard
-Speaker's platform

Arrange the diamonded letters to solve mystery answer #1. Arrange the circled letters to solve mystery answer #2.

(The mystery answers will relate to each other.)

MYSTERY ANSWER #1

MYSTERY ANSWER #2

ELEMENTS

JUMBLE BrainBusters

Unscramble the Jumbles, one letter to each square, to spell names of elements.

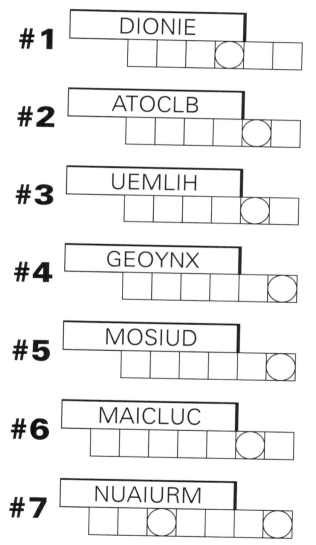

#1 DIONIE

#2 ATOCLB

#3 UEMLIH

#4 GEOYNX

#5 MOSIUD

#6 MAICLUC

#7 NUAIURM

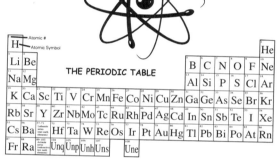

THE PERIODIC TABLE

Box of Clues

Stumped? Maybe you can find a clue below.

- Starts with *H*; ends with *M*
- Starts with *A*; ends with *M*
- Starts with *O*; ends with *N*
- Starts with *I*; ends with *E*
- Starts with *U*; ends with *M*
- Starts with *S*; ends with *M*
- Starts with *C*; ends with *M*
- Starts with *C*; ends with *T*

Arrange the circled letters to solve the mystery answer.

MYSTERY ANSWER

145

TRIPLE JUMBLE® BRAINBUSTERS

Unscramble the Jumbles, one letter to each square, to spell words.

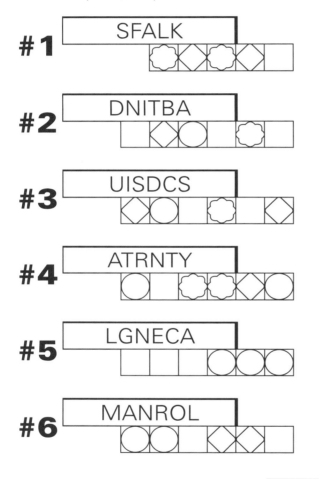

#1 SFALK

#2 DNITBA

#3 UISDCS

#4 ATRNTY

#5 LGNECA

#6 MANROL

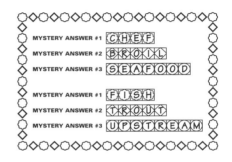

MYSTERY ANSWER #1 CHEF
MYSTERY ANSWER #2 BROIL
MYSTERY ANSWER #3 SEAFOOD

MYSTERY ANSWER #1 FISH
MYSTERY ANSWER #2 TROUT
MYSTERY ANSWER #3 UPSTREAM

Box of Clues

Stumped? Maybe you can find a clue below. (No clues for the mystery answers.)

- Oppressive ruler
- Average
- Container for liquid
- Thief
- Look
- Thrown circular plate

Arrange the clouded letters to solve mystery answer #1. Arrange the diamonded letters to solve mystery answer #2. Arrange the circled letters to solve mystery answer #3.
(The mystery answers will relate to each other.)

MYSTERY ANSWER #1

MYSTERY ANSWER #2

MYSTERY ANSWER #3

COUNTRIES

JUMBLE BrainBusters

Unscramble the Jumbles, one letter to each square, to spell names of countries.

#1 GINIARE

#2 SATIRUA

#3 AUUUYGR

#4 MEGYNRA

#5 COMOORC

#6 HETIOIAP

#7 ATDIHALN

Box of Clues

Stumped? Maybe you can find a clue below.

- Starts with *T*; ends with *D*
- Starts with *A*; ends with *A*
- Starts with *E*; ends with *A*
- Starts with *M*; ends with *R*
- Starts with *U*; ends with *Y*
- Starts with *G*; ends with *Y*
- Starts with *M*; ends with *O*
- Starts with *N*; ends with *A*

Arrange the circled letters to solve the mystery answer.

MYSTERY ANSWER

ADJECTIVES

JUMBLE BrainBusters

Unscramble the Jumbles, one letter to each square, to spell adjectives.

#1 BGBYA

#2 KAEAW

#3 SFIYTE

#4 TLUIYG

#5 RHIODR

#6 UDCYDL

#7 SCTMOU

#8 OMGOYL

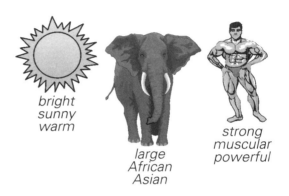

bright sunny warm

large African Asian

strong muscular powerful

Box of Clues

Stumped? Maybe you can find a clue below.

- Talkative
- Ghastly
- Cognizant
- Blameworthy
- Made-to-order
- Being touchy and quarrelsome
- Snugly
- Agreeable, pleasant, pleasing
- Sullen

Arrange the circled letters to solve the mystery answer.

MYSTERY ANSWER

ANTARCTICA

Unscramble the Jumbles, one letter
to each square, to spell words related
to Antarctica.

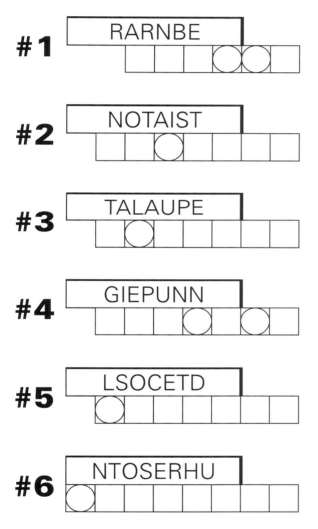

#1 RARNBE

#2 NOTAIST

#3 TALAUPE

#4 GIEPUNN

#5 LSOCETD

#6 NTOSERHU

ANTARCTICA

Box of Clues

Stumped? Maybe you can find a clue
below. (No clue for the mystery answer.)

-Adjective that describes
 Antarctica weather compared
 to all other continents
-Desolate
-Adjective that describes
 Antarctica that relates to
 direction and location
-Antarctica resident
-Extensive land area having a
 relatively level surface raised
 sharply above adjacent land
-Science _____

Arrange the circled letters
to solve the mystery answer.

MYSTERY ANSWER

BEST PICTURE
ACADEMY AWARD WINNERS

JUMBLE. BrainBusters

#1 KOYRC

#2 DAHIGN

#3 ANTICIT

#4 LAONOPT

#5 MIRANNA

#6 GNITETSH

#7 TLAIORAGD

#8 FUENGOVNIR

Unscramble the Jumbles, one letter to each square, to spell names of movies that won Best Picture Academy Awards.

Box of Clues

Stumped? Maybe you can find a clue below.

#1) 1976 Best Picture
#2) 1982 Best Picture
#3) 1997 Best Picture
#4) 1986 Best Picture
#5) 1988 Best Picture
#6) 1973 Best Picture
#7) 2000 Best Picture
#8) 1992 Best Picture
M.A.) 1972 Best Picture

Arrange the circled letters to solve the mystery answer.

MYSTERY ANSWER

OUTER SPACE

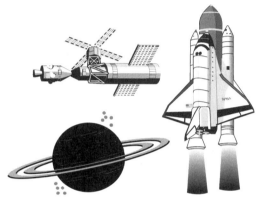

JUMBLE BrainBusters

Unscramble the Jumbles, one letter to each square, to spell words related to outer space.

#1 CAUMUV

#2 SCOOSM

#3 TARIYGV

#4 TPEURIJ

#5 PLIEECS

#6 OSSUTPN

Box of Clues

Stumped? Maybe you can find a clue below.

-Mars' outer neighbor
-Total _____
-Carl Sagan TV show
-Universal attractive force
-Entire celestial cosmos
-Empty space
-Disturbance on the sun's surface

Arrange the circled letters to solve the mystery answer.

MYSTERY ANSWER

ANIMALS

Unscramble the Jumbles, one letter to each square, to spell names of animals.

#1 OAKAL

#2 USOME

#3 LCJKAA

#4 ACOBTB

#5 EOCOTL

#6 TOSCIHR

#7 STOOIRET

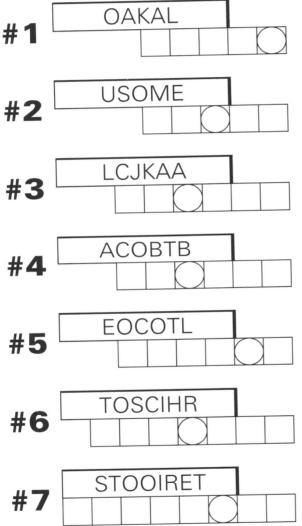

Box of Clues

Stumped? Maybe you can find a clue below.

-Starts with *B*; ends with *T*
-Starts with *C*; ends with *U*
-Starts with *M*; ends with *E*
-Starts with *K*; ends with *A*
-Starts with *T*; ends with *E*
-Starts with *O*; ends with *H*
-Starts with *J*; ends with *L*
-Starts with *O*; ends with *T*

Arrange the circled letters to solve the mystery answer.

MYSTERY ANSWER

DOUBLE JUMBLE® BRAINBUSTERS

Unscramble the Jumbles, one letter to each square, to spell words.

#1 SUMYH

#2 KPIELC

#3 RDGNEE

#4 OETCJB

#5 GUEOHN

#6 AIFYSFL

MYSTERY ANSWER #1 SUNNY
MYSTERY ANSWER #2 WEATHER

MYSTERY ANSWER #1 SPORTS
MYSTERY ANSWER #2 ATHLETES

MYSTERY ANSWER #1 COUNTRY
MYSTERY ANSWER #2 ETHIOPIA

Box of Clues

Stumped? Maybe you can find a clue below. (No clues for the mystery answers.)

- Problem
- Emotional
- Plenty
- Thing
- Male, for example
- Misrepresent

Arrange the diamonded letters to solve mystery answer #1. Arrange the circled letters to solve mystery answer #2.
(The mystery answers will relate to each other.)

MYSTERY ANSWER #1

MYSTERY ANSWER #2

STARTS WITH S

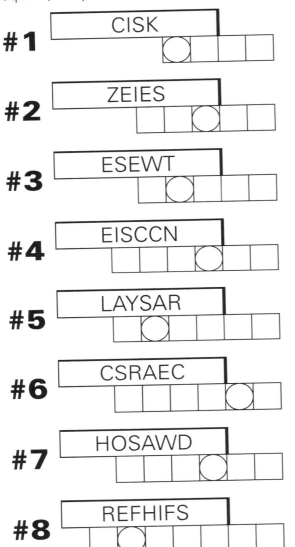

Unscramble the Jumbles, one letter to each square, to spell words that start with *S*.

#1 CISK

#2 ZEIES

#3 ESEWT

#4 EISCCN

#5 LAYSAR

#6 CSRAEC

#7 HOSAWD

#8 REFHIFS

Arrange the circled letters
to solve the mystery answer.

JUMBLE
BrainBusters

Box of Clues

Stumped? Maybe you can find a clue below.

-_____ spot
-Andy Griffith role
-Beautiful
-_____ leave
-Deficient in quantity or number compared with the demand
-Grab
-Fixed compensation paid regularly for services
-Eye _____
-Club, for example

MYSTERY ANSWER

SUPER JUMBLE® CHALLENGE

JUMBLE® BrainBusters

#1 ITB

Unscramble the Jumbles, one letter to each square, to spell words.

#2 NUPT

#3 NFAIL

#4 CSEDON

#5 NTSOEVL

#6 CIELITPX

#7 CFILEENNU

#8 RMEUONDMAM

#9 AREINBRGEDG

#10 USONTINTIOCT

Box of Clues

Stumped? Maybe you can find a clue below.

- Directive note
- Small time increment
- Able to pay all legal debts
- Act of giving the proper sound and accent
- Type of kick
- Small morsel
- Important document
- _____ man
- Affect
- Closing
- Fully revealed

Arrange the circled letters to solve the mystery answer.

MYSTERY ANSWER

JUMBLE BrainBusters

SPORTS

Unscramble the Jumbles, one letter to each square, to spell words related to sports.

#1 OHRME

#2 GNININ

#3 ELUAEG

#4 NOESSA

#5 BRDILEB

#6 KREICTC

#7 YTIVCOR

#8 NACAIPT

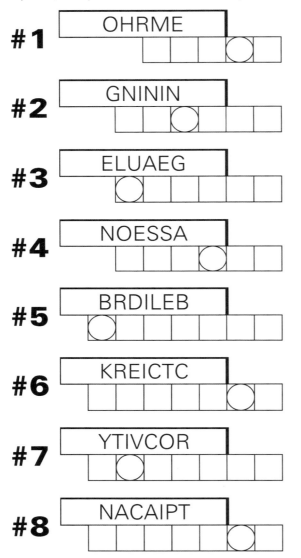

Box of Clues

Stumped? Maybe you can find a clue below.

- _____ tickets
- Basketball action
- Reason for a batter to trot
- An increment made up of a "top" and a "bottom"
- Edge of area of play
- NFL's "L"
- Game played with a ball and bat by two sides of usually 11 players each
- Team leader
- Win

Arrange the circled letters to solve the mystery answer.

MYSTERY ANSWER

PLANET EARTH

Unscramble the Jumbles, one letter to each square, to spell words related to planet Earth.

#1 ACEHB

#2 SARGS

#3 NDURTA

#4 NYNOAC

#5 UNRODG

#6 TLIEMCA

#7 TLEAUPA

Arrange the circled letters to solve the mystery answer.

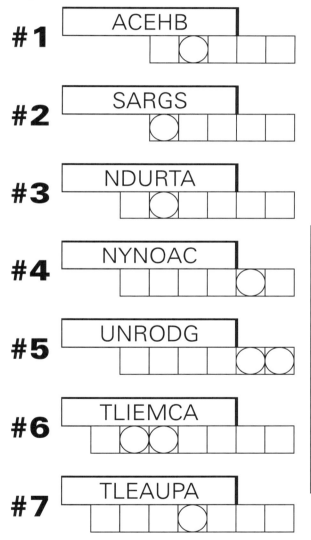

Interesting Planet Earth Facts

Venezuela's Angel Falls is one mile high.

The average life expectancy of a white ash tree is 275 years.

The African baobab tree can have a circumference as large as 100 feet.

MYSTERY ANSWER

MYSTERY PERSON

JUMBLE BrainBusters

Unscramble the Jumbles, one letter to each square, to spell words that relate to the mystery person.

#1 CAAIFR

#2 LUEGJN

#3 TOPOSH

#4 GAELDNN

#5 ANNATIAZ

#6 BGCRIEDMA

Box of Clues

Use the clues below to help you solve the six Jumbles.

- Continent on which most of her work is carried out
- Tropical forest
- Her birthplace
- She founded a research center in this country
- She received a Ph.D. from this university
- You'll see these in the many books she's published

Arrange the circled letters to solve the mystery person.

MYSTERY PERSON

MOVIES

Unscramble the Jumbles, one letter to each square, to spell names of movies.

#1 SGOTH

#2 BMDOU

#3 ACIOSN

#4 KCPBAAY

#5 NNARIMA

#6 AMNAOIGL

#7 OTGAIARDL

Box of Clues

Stumped? Maybe you can find a clue below.

- 1999 Mel Gibson movie
- 1990 haunting romance
- 1995 movie set in Las Vegas
- 1998 award-winning movie about two brothers
- 2000 movie set thousands of years ago
- 1993 Bill Murray movie
- 1941 movie about a large mammal
- 1999 movie that shares its name with a tree

Arrange the circled letters to solve the mystery answer.

MYSTERY ANSWER

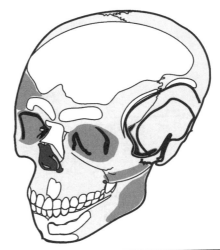

THE HUMAN BODY

Unscramble the Jumbles, one letter to each square, to spell words related to the human body.

#1 ESHTC

#2 LFIAUB

#3 EESNLP

#4 RAHTOT

#5 GEOTUN

#6 CTAEAHR

#7 RAOEMFR

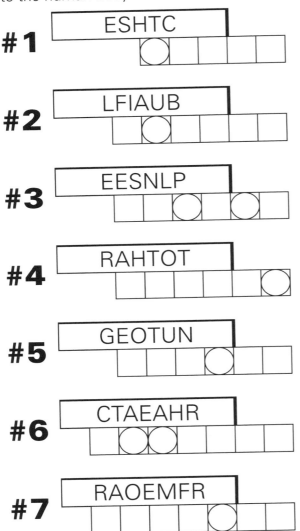

Arrange the circled letters to solve the mystery answer.

Box of Clues

Stumped? Maybe you can find a clue below.

-Starts with *F*; ends with *A*
-Starts with *T*; ends with *A*
-Starts with *T*; ends with *E*
-Starts with *S*; ends with *N*
-Starts with *T*; ends with *T*
-Starts with *C*; ends with *E*
-Starts with *C*; ends with *T*
-Starts with *F*; ends with *M*

MYSTERY ANSWER

MATH

Unscramble the Jumbled letters, one letter to each square, so that each equation is correct.

For example: NONTEOEOW
ONE + ONE = TWO

#1 RTUGEIOFOWTH

○□□□□□ ÷ ○□□○ = ○□□□

#2 RNEFIEOTUWTYVF

□□□□□ × □□□□□ = ○□○□□□

#3 NESIOIEODSZXNX

□□□□ + □□□□ = □□○ □○□□□

#4 RTNSISEETHIENXEV

□○□ + □□○○□ = □○□○□□□□

#5 TOEDNUTHRDENENEN

□□○ ○□□□□○ ÷ □□○ = □□□

Then arrange the circled letters to solve the mystery equation.

MYSTERY EQUATION

○○○ + ○○○○ = ○○○○○ + ○○○○○

MEANS THE OPPOSITE

JUMBLE BrainBusters

Unscramble the Jumbles, one letter to each square, to spell pairs of words that have opposite or nearly opposite meanings.

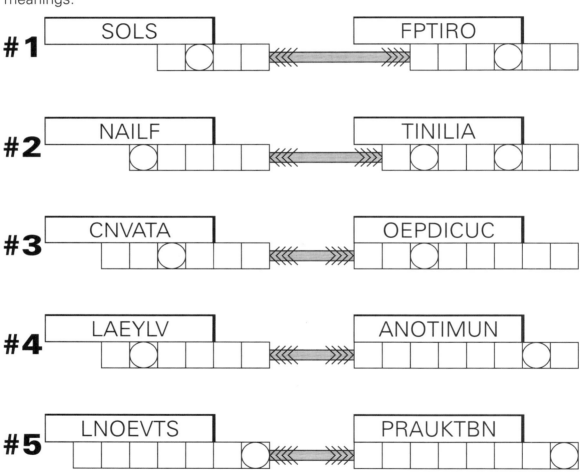

#1 SOLS FPTIRO

#2 NAILF TINILIA

#3 CNVATA OEPDICUC

#4 LAEYLV ANOTIMUN

#5 LNOEVTS PRAUKTBN

Arrange the circled letters to solve the mystery answer.
(Form two words that have the opposite or nearly opposite meanings.)

MYSTERY ANSWER

BIRDS

JUMBLE® BrainBusters

Unscramble the Jumbles, one letter to each square, to spell words related to birds.

#1 ERVNA

#2 REOPYS

#3 GAMIEP

#4 TRULEVU

#5 RLAMLDA

#6 RBBEIDLU

#7 DCAINLAR

#8 KOOCOTCA

Box of Clues

Stumped? Maybe you can find a clue below. (No clue for the mystery answer.)

-Common wild duck
-Jay relative but having a long, graduated tail and black-and-white or brightly colored plumage
-Large, glossy black bird
-Circling raptor
-Large, raptorial bird
-Small North American thrush
-Crested finch
-Noisy parrot

Arrange the circled letters to solve the mystery answer.

MYSTERY ANSWER

TRIPLE JUMBLE® BRAINBUSTERS

Unscramble the Jumbles, one letter to each square, to spell words.

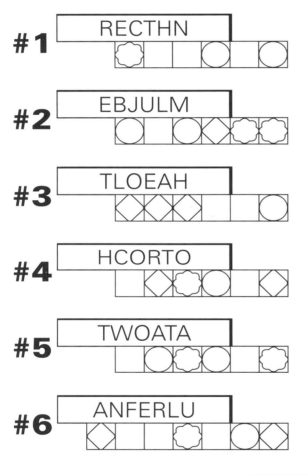

#1 RECTHN

#2 EBJULM

#3 TLOEAH

#4 HCORTO

#5 TWOATA

#6 ANFERLU

MYSTERY ANSWER #1 C H E F
MYSTERY ANSWER #2 B R O I L
MYSTERY ANSWER #3 S E A F O O D

MYSTERY ANSWER #1 F I S H
MYSTERY ANSWER #2 T R O U T
MYSTERY ANSWER #3 U P S T R E A M

Box of Clues

Stumped? Maybe you can find a clue below. (No clues for the mystery answers.)

- _____ home
- Capital of Canada
- _____ coat
- Mix up
- Colleague
- Despise

Arrange the clouded letters to solve mystery answer #1. Arrange the diamonded letters to solve mystery answer #2. Arrange the circled letters to solve mystery answer #3.
(The mystery answers will relate to each other.)

MYSTERY ANSWER #1

MYSTERY ANSWER #2

MYSTERY ANSWER #3

WARS AND THE MILITARY

JUMBLE BrainBusters

Unscramble the Jumbles, one letter to each square, to spell words related to wars and the military.

#1 AOCNNN

#2 RFOIEFC

#3 MAIRLAD

#4 RAISUAM

#5 TLFOIALL

#6 NRPSERIO

#7 GAEOPTNN

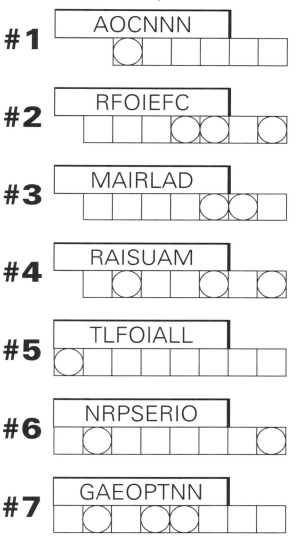

Box of Clues

Stumped? Maybe you can find a clue below.

- _____ of war
- Large, heavy gun
- Fleet of warships
- Rear _____
- Commissioned _____
- Japanese warrior
- A large warship
- Home of U.S. military leadership

Arrange the circled letters to solve the mystery answer.

MYSTERY ANSWER

ACTORS & ACTRESSES

JUMBLE BrainBusters

Unscramble the Jumbles, one letter to each square, to spell names of actors and actresses.

#1 MDIE ORMOE

#2 EREN USORS

#3 NIBG RBSYCO

#4 RMKA MLAILH

#5 VKINE NKEIL

#6 ENLNG LCEOS

Box of Clues

Stumped? Maybe you can find a clue below.

- *Star Wars* star
- *A Fish Called Wanda* star
- *Tin Cup* star
- *Fatal Attraction* star
- *Disclosure* star
- *Hamlet* star
- *Road to Morocco* star

Arrange the circled letters to solve the mystery answer.

MYSTERY ANSWER

SEWING

JUMBLE BrainBusters

Unscramble the Jumbles, one letter to each square, to spell words related to sewing.

#1 BFAICR

#2 EEDENL

#3 TOUTNB

#4 MLTIEHB

#5 HNACEIM

#6 SRSISOSC

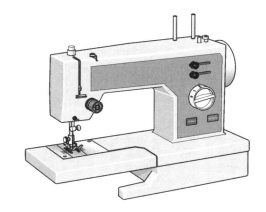

Box of Clues

Stumped? Maybe you can find a clue below.

-Starts with *S*; ends with *S*
-Starts with *B*; ends with *N*
-Starts with *F*; ends with *C*
-Starts with *M*; ends with *E*
-Starts with *A*; ends with *N*
-Starts with *T*; ends with *E*
-Starts with *N*; ends with *E*

Arrange the circled letters to solve the mystery answer.

MYSTERY ANSWER

TRIPLE JUMBLE® BRAINBUSTERS

Unscramble the Jumbles, one letter to each square, to spell words.

#1 FSITW

#2 FHIYST

#3 KWEIDC

#4 DESADL

#5 EYLWRA

#6 ROTNIOA

#7 ESAIAMN

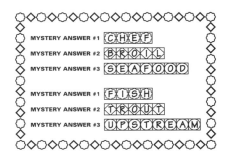

MYSTERY ANSWER #1 C H E F
MYSTERY ANSWER #2 B R O I L
MYSTERY ANSWER #3 S E A F O O D

MYSTERY ANSWER #1 F I S H
MYSTERY ANSWER #2 T R O U T
MYSTERY ANSWER #3 U P S T R E A M

Box of Clues

Stumped? Maybe you can find a clue below. (No clues for the mystery answers.)

- Attorney
- Elusive, tricky
- _____ sore
- Forgetful condition
- Fast
- Mean
- Canadian province

Arrange the clouded letters to solve mystery answer #1. Arrange the diamonded letters to solve mystery answer #2. Arrange the circled letters to solve mystery answer #3.
(The mystery answers will relate to each other.)

MYSTERY ANSWER #1

MYSTERY ANSWER #2

MYSTERY ANSWER #3

WEATHER

Unscramble the Jumbles, one letter to each square, to spell words related to weather.

#1 LFEKA

#2 LOFDO

#3 EREGDSE

#4 BIROWNA

#5 NOOMOSN

#6 LARILANF

#7 DTUIHIYM

#8 WOPUDNRO

Box of Clues

Stumped? Maybe you can find a clue below.

-_____ watch or warning
-Beautiful weather phenomenon
-Snow formation
-Storm's type of compression
-Major wind system that
 seasonally reverses its direction
-Amount of liquid precipitation
-Heavy rain
-Relative _____
-Temperature units

Arrange the circled letters to solve the mystery answer.

MYSTERY ANSWER

U.S. PRESIDENTS

Unscramble the Jumbles, one letter to each square, to spell the first and last names of U.S. presidents.

#1 TMHRARRUNYA

#2 EJMMSNROEAO

#3 NROIADINHXCR

#4 MOSJAADSINME

#5 LRDAEJEAFIGMS

#6 NSNLDNOOHONJY

#7 ANHRNERRIGAWD

Arrange the circled letters to solve the mystery answer.

MYSTERY ANSWER

QUADRUPLE JUMBLE BRAINBUSTERS

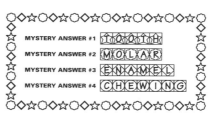

Unscramble the Jumbles, one letter to each square, to spell words.

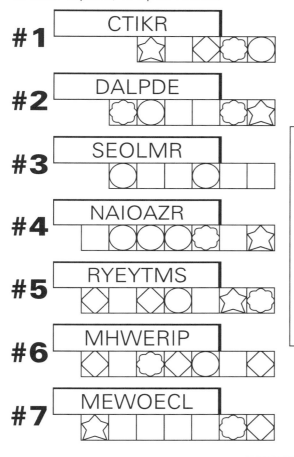

#1 CTIKR

#2 DALPDE

#3 SEOLMR

#4 NAIOAZR

#5 RYEYTMS

#6 MHWERIP

#7 MEWOECL

MYSTERY ANSWER #1 TOOTH
MYSTERY ANSWER #2 MOLAR
MYSTERY ANSWER #3 ENAMEL
MYSTERY ANSWER #4 CHEWING

Box of Clues

Stumped? Maybe you can find a clue below.
(No clues for the mystery answers.)

-Bit, fragment
-Prank
-Ping Pong _____
-Low, whining sound
-_____ mat
-Enigma
-One of 50

Arrange the starred letters to solve mystery answer #1. Arrange the clouded letters to solve mystery answer #2. Arrange the diamonded letters to solve mystery answer #3. Arrange the circled letters to solve mystery answer #4.
(The mystery answers will relate to each other.)

MYSTERY ANSWER #1

MYSTERY ANSWER #2

MYSTERY ANSWER #3

MYSTERY ANSWER #4

TRIPLE JUMBLE® BRAINBUSTERS

Unscramble the Jumbles, one letter to each square, to spell words.

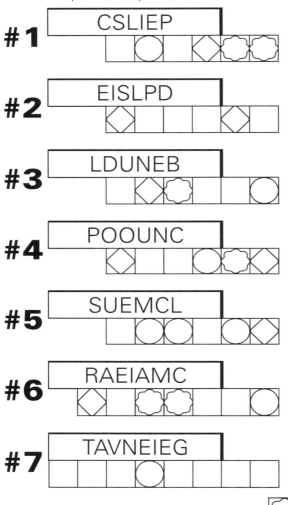

#1 CSLIEP

#2 EISLPD

#3 LDUNEB

#4 POOUNC

#5 SUEMCL

#6 RAEIAMC

#7 TAVNEIEG

MYSTERY ANSWER #1

MYSTERY ANSWER #2

MYSTERY ANSWER #3

JUMBLE BrainBusters

MYSTERY ANSWER #1 C H E F
MYSTERY ANSWER #2 B R O I L
MYSTERY ANSWER #3 S E A F O O D

MYSTERY ANSWER #1 F I S H
MYSTERY ANSWER #2 T R O U T
MYSTERY ANSWER #3 U P S T R E A M

Box of Clues

Stumped? Maybe you can find a clue below. (No clues for the mystery answers.)

-Drive away
-South _____
-Group of things fastened together
-Unite
-_____ feedback
-Discount certificate
-_____-bound

Arrange the clouded letters to solve mystery answer #1. Arrange the diamonded letters to solve mystery answer #2. Arrange the circled letters to solve mystery answer #3.
(The mystery answers will relate to each other.)

MATH

JUMBLE BrainBusters

Unscramble the Jumbled
letters, one letter to each square,
so that each equation is correct.

For example: NOLSOEPNEU
ONE PLUS ONE = TWO

#1 RTWEOTIOSWOFUMT

☐☐◯ ☐☐◯☐ ☐☐◯ = ◯☐☐☐

#2 NTEPNLTSENTWEYTU

☐◯☐ ☐◯☐☐ ☐☐☐ = ☐☐☐◯☐

#3 NFPVIUELSIELSEVXE

☐☐◯☐ ☐☐☐☐ ◯☐☐ = ☐☐☐◯☐

#4 GREITIMNHSUEITEOGZH

☐☐☐◯☐ ☐☐☐◯☐ ☐◯☐☐ = ☐◯☐☐

#5 NXNIELNPSUEESVIETNES

☐☐☐◯ ☐☐☐☐ ☐☐☐◯ = ◯☐☐☐☐

Then arrange the
circled letters to solve
the mystery equation.

MYSTERY EQUATION

◯◯◯◯◯ ◯◯◯◯◯ ◯◯◯ = ◯◯◯◯

173

SUPER JUMBLE® CHALLENGE

JUMBLE BrainBusters

#1 NMA

Unscramble the Jumbles, one letter to each square, to spell words.

#2 LIPL

#3 UGVOE

#4 RFIEEC

#5 MGRRAPO

#6 CLUAKOTB

#7 CRITSETNE

#8 AKAMCHERMT

#9 TANUNPUIOTC

#10 ONDAMIUNSIET

Box of Clues

Stumped? Maybe you can find a clue below.

-Date arranger
-In fashion
-A period of darkness
-Logical ski cabin position
-Male human
-Form, shape
-Windows or Excel
-Meet and cross
-_____ mark
-Tablet
-Barbarous

Arrange the circled letters to solve the mystery answer.

MYSTERY ANSWER

MYSTERY PERSON

JUMBLE BrainBusters

Unscramble the Jumbles, one letter to each square, to spell words that relate to the mystery person.

#1 RVHRADA

#2 ENIEENNT

#3 RWOTAESF

#4 FSICOORTM

#5 SHTELTIAEW

#6 GONWITNAHS

#7 ARNILIOIEBL

Arrange the circled letters to solve the mystery person.

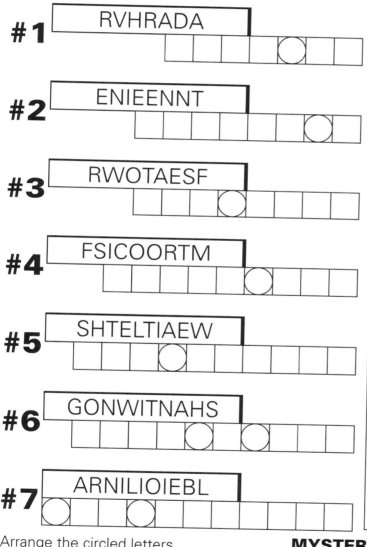

Box of Clues

Use the clues below to help you solve the seven Jumbles.

- He was born in this U.S. state
- He attended this prestigious college
- Age at which he dropped out of college
- Adjective that describes his money situation
- This person is one many times over
- A product created by this person
- Company started by this person

MYSTERY PERSON

ANIMAL RELATED WORDS

Unscramble the Jumbles, one letter to each square, to spell words related to animals.

#1 NFEIEL

#2 NIANEC

#3 RSUYCR

#4 GOFAER

#5 RVIENM

#6 AMMLMA

#7 ETCIRRT

#8 CPEISSE

Box of Clues

Stumped? Maybe you can find a clue below. (No clue for the mystery answer.)

- Wander in search of food
- Small, common, harmful or objectionable animals
- Endangered _____
- Cat's group
- Dog's group
- Creature, animal
- An elephant but not a lizard
- Surprised animal's retreating action

Arrange the circled letters to solve the mystery answer.

MYSTERY ANSWER

TV SHOWS

Unscramble the Jumbles, one letter
to each square, to spell names of
TV shows.

#1 AITX

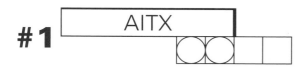

#2 CLIEA

#3 THELO

#4 SBOYC

#7 EHESCR

#5 ALDASL

#8 RPLIEFP

#6 TUEHRN

#9 UMOLOCB

Arrange the circled
letters to solve the
mystery answer.

MYSTERY ANSWER

MILITARY

JUMBLE BrainBusters

Unscramble the Jumbles, one letter to each square, to spell words related to war and the military.

#1 ANYV

#2 OMBB

#3 LULTBE

#4 CATAKT

#5 KEOCRT

#6 MEETLH

#7 RFUIGNE

#8 EPHORPC

#9 MIRLADA

Arrange the circled letters to solve the mystery answer.

MYSTERY ANSWER

STATE CAPITALS

JUMBLE BrainBusters

Unscramble the Jumbles, one letter to each square, to spell names of state capitals.

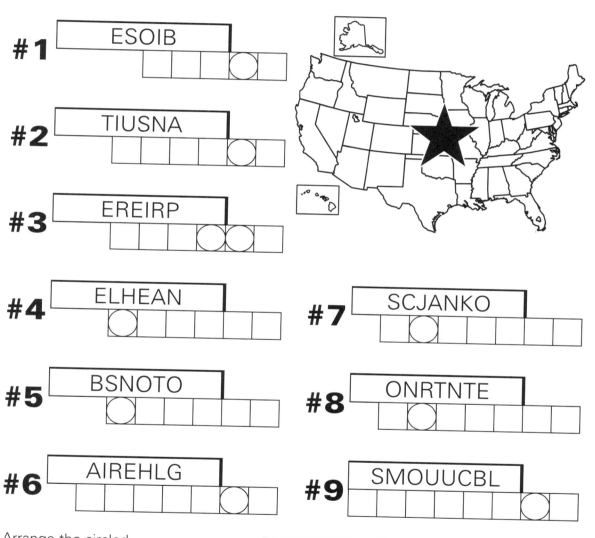

#1 ESOIB

#2 TIUSNA

#3 EREIRP

#4 ELHEAN

#5 BSNOTO

#6 AIREHLG

#7 SCJANKO

#8 ONRTNTE

#9 SMOUUCBL

Arrange the circled letters to solve the mystery answer.

MYSTERY ANSWER

PUZZLE 177

MUSIC

JUMBLE. BrainBusters

Unscramble the Jumbles, one letter to each square, to spell words related to music.

#1 RHPA

#2 NPAIO

#3 TAURIG

#4 DELYMO

#5 LCPIOOC

#6 RONTCCE

#7 OSAOSNB

#8 SUERMAE

#9 DOANINML

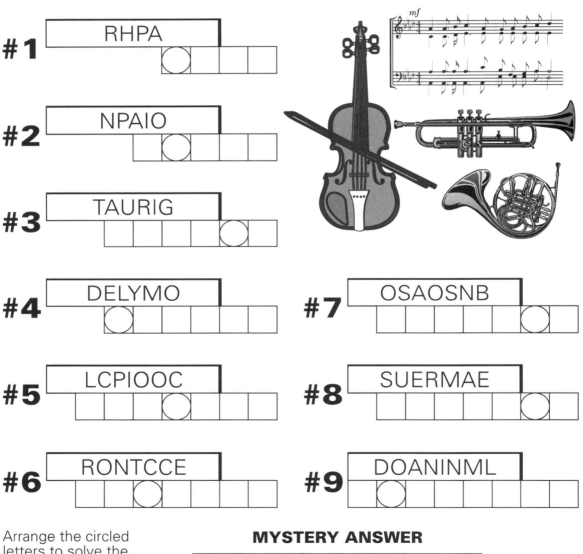

Arrange the circled letters to solve the mystery answer.

MYSTERY ANSWER

ANIMALS

Unscramble the Jumbles, one letter to each square, to spell words related to animals.

#1 KNUSK

#2 SOEGO

#3 NIOEPG

#4 RETREF

#5 LKACJA

#6 AESELW

#7 ULRWSA

#8 GIEUNNP

#9 EHTANRP

Arrange the circled letters to solve the mystery answer.

MYSTERY ANSWER

ANSWERS

1. **Jumbles:** #1. AGILE #2. OPERA #3. IMAGE #4. IGUANA #5. EUREKA #6. INCOME #7. ADVANCE
Answer: AVERAGE

2. **Jumbles:** #1. DUCK #2. TIGER #3. RHINO #4. SKUNK #5. PANDA #6. TURTLE
Answer: PENGUIN

3. **Jumbles:** #1. A WATCH DOG #2. FROSTBITE #3. CELL PHONES #4. A VOLLEYBALL #5. A BALD EAGLE #6. A PUDDLE #7. FAST FOOD

4. **Jumbles:** #1. PUCK #2. COACH #3. TENNIS #4. SOCCER #5. REFEREE #6. UNIFORM
Answer: PRACTICE

5. **Jumbles:** #1. FILM #2. CHAIR #3. SCRIPT #4. CASTING #5. COSTUME #6. LOCATION
Answer: STUNTMEN

6. **Jumbles:** #1. FAKE #2. FRILL #3. FABLE #4. FINISH #5. FABRIC #6. FLUFFY #7. FORMAL #8. FORMULA
Answer: FABULOUS

7. **Jumbles:** #1. DALLAS, TEXAS #2. MIAMI, FLORIDA #3. ATLANTA, GEORGIA #4. DENVER, COLORADO #5. PORTLAND, OREGON #6. DETROIT, MICHIGAN
Answer: CLEVELAND, OHIO

8. **Jumbles:** #1. SHIRT #2. PARKA #3. JEANS #4. SCARF #5. JACKET #6. MITTEN
Answer: SNEAKERS

9. **Jumbles:** #1. SIX + ZERO = SIX #2. FIVE – THREE = TWO #3. SEVEN – FIVE = TWO #4. NINE + TWO = ELEVEN #5. FOUR + FOUR = EIGHT
Answer: ONE + EIGHT = NINE

10. **Jumbles:** #1. SOAP #2. MAUDE #3. CHEERS #4. CANNON #5. NEWHART #6. JEOPARDY
Answer: MY THREE SONS

11. **Jumbles:** #1. TELL—RELATE #2. TRIP—JOURNEY #3. CHILD—YOUTH #4. EMPTY—HOLLOW #5. GLOOM—SADNESS
Answer: GLAD—HAPPY

12. **Jumbles:** #1. UNIT #2. NAVY #3. BOMB #4. RADAR #5. WEAPON #6. MISSION
Answer: INVASION

13. **Jumbles:** #1. WAITER #2. JANITOR #3. REALTOR #4. SURVEYOR #5. PHYSICIAN #6. CARPENTER
Answer: JOURNALIST

14. **Jumbles:** #1. PATTON #2. MISERY #3. TOOTSIE #4. THE FIRM #5. THE BIRDS #6. THE STING #7. THE MUMMY
Answer: FORREST GUMP

15. **Jumbles:** #1. DIRTY #2. COMFY #3. DECENT #4. FLABBY #5. FROSTY #6. CLUMSY
Answer: FORCEFUL

16. **Jumbles:** #1. GARDEN #2. LAUNDRY #3. ERRANDS #4. STRESS #5. TODAY
Answer: DELAY

17. **Jumbles:** #1. MILD #2. DAMP #3. FLAKE #4. RADAR #5. HUMID #6. STORM #7. BREEZE #8. THUNDER
Answer: TEMPERATURE

18. **Jumbles:** #1. NED BEATTY #2. TOM CRUISE #3. WILL SMITH #4. LILY TOMLIN #5. SALLY FIELD #6. ROGER MOORE
Answer: WOODY ALLEN

19. **Jumbles:** #1. MAINE #2. GEORGIA #3. WYOMING #4. MONTANA #5. NEBRASKA #6. COLORADO
Answer: DELAWARE

20. **Jumble:** DID YOU KNOW THAT TOM CRUISE LEFT SEMINARY SCHOOL TO BECOME AN ACTOR? IT'S TRUE. HE DROPPED OUT AT AGE 18 AND HEADED TO NEW YORK CITY TO ACT.
Answer: RAIN MAN

21. **Jumbles:** #1. TAFT #2. GRANT #3. ADAMS #4. HOOVER #5. JOHNSON #6. GARFIELD
Answer: JEFFERSON

22. **Jumbles:** #1. GUIDE #2. POLICY #3. LARYNX #4. PUPPET #5. REVOKE #6. ALMOST
Answers: #1. COLOR #2. PURPLE

23. **Jumbles:** #1. BALL #2. FRED #3. RICKY #4. ARNAZ #5. CUBAN #6. SITCOM
Answer: RICARDO

24. **Jumbles:** #1. PORCH #2. SIDING #3. PANTRY #4. FAUCET #5. GARAGE #6. CHIMNEY #7. PLUMBING
Answer: ELECTRICITY

25. **Jumbles:** #1. ITALY #2. RUSSIA #3. BRAZIL #4. CANADA #5. GREECE #6. MEXICO #7. IRELAND
Answer: AUSTRALIA

26. **Jumbles:** #1. LAZY—HAZY #2. BELL—SELL #3. CAVE—WAVE #4. CHIEF—THIEF #5. CLASSY—GRASSY
Answer: CALL—TALL

27. **Jumbles:** #1. AUSTIN #2. BOSTON #3. LANSING #4. JACKSON #5. BISMARCK #6. HONOLULU
Answer: COLUMBUS

28. **Jumbles:** #1. HOOK #2. DIVOT #3. EAGLE #4. BIRDIE #5. DIMPLES #6. ADDRESS #7. SCOTLAND #8. MULLIGAN
Answer: THE MASTERS

29. **Jumbles:** #1. HUBBY #2. TALLER #3. JUGGLE #4. MUFFIN #5. MIDDLE #6. BOGGLE #7. PUMMEL
Answer: BULLDOG

30. **Jumbles:** #1. DECAY #2. FLOSS #3. CROWN #4. CAVITY #5. FILLING #6. EXTRACT
Answer: NOVOCAIN

31. **Jumbles:** #1. GRILL #2. LUNCH #3. SNACK #4. FUDGE #5. GARLIC #6. CHEESE #7. BLENDER
Answer: SIDE DISH

32. **Jumbles:** #1. MULE #2. MOLE #3. HYENA #4. GOOSE #5. TURKEY #6. COUGAR
Answer: COYOTE

33. **Jumbles:** #1. BLUFF #2. CRUST #3. GLOBE #4. ISLAND #5. SEASON #6. GLACIER #7. EQUATOR
Answer: RAIN FOREST

34. **Jumbles:** #1. LIVID #2. LAUGH #3. FINALE #4. HORRID #5. PALACE #6. GLOSSY
Answers: #1. CLOUDY #2. RAINFALL

35. **Jumbles:** #1. A FENCE #2. ROOT CANAL #3. THEY CHARGE #4. TWISTER #5. GROUND BEEF #6. A YARDSTICK #7. ONE SCENT

36. **Jumbles:** #1. SAFELY #2. NOISILY #3. LIGHTLY #4. BRIEFLY #5. CLEARLY #6. LOOSELY
Answer: HASTILY

37. **Jumbles:** #1. FUN #2. HAWK #3. TRACK #4. FOURTH #5. COMPACT #6. EGGPLANT #7. GLADIATOR #8. INCREDIBLE #9. PUBLICATION #10. DISADVANTAGE
Answer: INTERNATIONAL

38. **Jumbles:** #1. MADONNA #2. LIBERACE #3. ROY CLARK #4. BILLY JOEL #5. RINGO STARR #6. JOHN DENVER
Answer: ELTON JOHN

39. **Jumbles:** #1. HABIT #2. HAVOC #3. HUMAN #4. HERMIT #5. HAGGLE #6. HAMMER #7. HAIRCUT #8. HAMSTER
Answer: HERITAGE

40. **Jumbles:** #1. KOALA #2. PIGEON #3. JAGUAR #4. GOPHER #5. WEASEL #6. WALRUS
Answer: GORILLA

41. **Jumbles:** #1. CUBA #2. INDIA #3. FRANCE #4. NORWAY #5. BOLIVIA #6. FINLAND #7. BERMUDA
Answer: COLOMBIA

42. **Jumbles:** #1. JUNEAU, ALASKA #2. HOUSTON, TEXAS #3. MOBILE, ALABAMA #4. PHOENIX, ARIZONA #5. ORLANDO, FLORIDA #6. PORTLAND, OREGON
Answer: BOISE, IDAHO

43. **Jumbles:** #1. ROBIN #2. STORK #3. GOOSE #4. PIGEON #5. TURKEY #6. CANARY #7. OSTRICH #8. FLAMINGO
Answer: PHEASANT

44. **Jumbles:** #1. JOIST #2. PERMIT #3. WIRING #4. CEMENT #5. HAMMER #6. PLYWOOD #7. WINDOWS
Answer: SHINGLES

45. **Jumbles:** #1. CAVE—BRAVE #2. MOSS—CROSS #3. JINGLE—SINGLE #4. SNOOZE—CHOOSE #5. BUCKLE—CHUCKLE
Answer: SICK—BRICK

46. **Jumbles:** #1. COMET #2. URANUS #3. GALAXY #4. APOLLO #5. NEPTUNE #6. MERCURY
Answer: ASTRONOMY

47. **Jumbles:** #1. ALIENS #2. TOP GUN #3. VERTIGO #4. TRAFFIC #5. DIE HARD #6. KING KONG #7. HIGH NOON
Answer: THE FUGITIVE

48. **Jumbles:** #1. SONG #2. PIANO #3. CHORD #4. DRUMS #5. TEMPO #6. GUITAR #7. CORNET
Answer: CONCERT

49. **Jumbles:** #1. PULL—PUSH #2. ROUGH—SMOOTH #3. VANISH—APPEAR #4. RANDOM—ORDERED #5. CROOKED—STRAIGHT
Answer: RICH—POOR

50. **Jumbles:** #1. SHOVE #2. PUTRID #3. GAGGLE #4. COFFEE #5. JARGON #6. SPRAWL
Answers: #1. GOLFER #2. TIGER WOODS

51. **Jumbles:** #1. BRAIN #2. ANKLE #3. BLOOD #4. PELVIS #5. KIDNEY #6. ENAMEL #7. EARDRUM
Answer: EPIDERMIS

52. **Jumbles:** #1. HOAX—TRICK #2. ABHOR—LOATHE #3. REJECT—REFUSE #4. SYMBOL—EMBLEM #5. BORDER—OUTLINE
Answer: LIFT—HOIST

53. **Jumbles:** #1. BASE #2. ARMOR #3. BULLET #4. DEFECT #5. OFFICER #6. VETERAN
Answer: SURRENDER

54. **Jumbles:** #1. CASH #2. LOAN #3. EURO #4. VAULT #5. PENNY #6. LENDER #7. CHANGE #8. DOLLAR
Answer: CURRENCY

55. **Jumbles:** #1. SKIING #2. TRIPLE #3. BOXING #4. PENALTY #5. OFFENSE #6. PLAYOFF
Answer: OPPONENT

56. **Jumbles:** #1. GOLDFISH #2. BLACKOUT #3. CREAMERY #4. BLUEPRINT #5. GREENBACK #6. BROWNSTONE
Answer: BLUEGRASS

57. **Jumbles:** #1. BYTE #2. MENU #3. VIRUS #4. MODEM #5. LAPTOP #6. FORMAT #7. PROGRAM #8. INTERNET
Answer: DATABASE

58. **Jumbles:** #1. IGLOO #2. ADAGE #3. ALPHA #4. ANKLE #5. ACTIVE #6. ENGINE #7. UTOPIA
Answer: ATHLETE

59. **Jumbles:** #1. THICK #2. PATCH #3. SKUNK #4. GUESS #5. HONEY #6. CROWN #7. SCATTER
Answer: SHUTTER

60. **Jumbles:** #1. DOCK #2. CREW #3. CASINO #4. VESSEL #5. GALLEY #6. BUFFET #7. VOYAGE #8. CAPTAIN
Answer: PORT OF CALL

61. **Jumbles:** #1. ALPHA #2. ADAMS #3. JANUARY #4. MERCURY #5. HYDROGEN
Answer: SUNDAY

62. **Jumbles:** #1. PILOT #2. NURSE #3. COACH #4. BARBER #5. JEWELLER #6. PLUMBER
Answer: CARPENTER

63. **Jumbles:** #1. JAPAN #2. FANCY #3. FORCE #4. MEDIC #5. SPIRIT #6. PAROLE
Answers: #1. JAIL #2. INMATE #3. PRISONER

64. **Jumbles:** #1. TAXI #2. YOGI #3. KHAKI #4. SAMURAI #5. ZUCCHINI #6. SHANGHAI
Answer: MACARONI

65. **Jumbles:** #1. ZINC #2. IRON #3. GOLD #4. COBALT #5. HELIUM #6. COPPER #7. HYDROGEN
Answer: NITROGEN

66. **Jumbles:** #1. LIMA, PERU #2. ROME, ITALY #3. CAIRO, EGYPT #4. BOMBAY, INDIA #5. WARSAW #6. TORONTO, CANADA
Answer: MADRID, SPAIN

67. **Jumbles:** #1. FISHY #2. EERIE #3. FUNNY #4. FURRY #5. EMPTY #6. BRIGHT #7. CRABBY
Answer: EFFICIENT

68. **Jumbles:** #1. FORD #2. REAGAN #3. LINCOLN #4. CLINTON #5. JACKSON #6. HARRISON
Answer: COOLIDGE

69. **Jumbles:** #1. HUNTER #2. FAMILY #3. BENSON #4. FRASIER #5. DYNASTY #6. MATLOCK #7. COLUMBO
Answer: BARNEY MILLER

70. **Jumbles:** #1. SUEDE #2. RAISIN #3. SHRINE #4. DALLAS #5. LEAGUE #6. HUMBLE
Answers: #1. ISLAND #2. BERMUDA

71. **Jumbles:** #1. HOOF #2. FARM #3. STALL #4. HANDS #5. SADDLE #6. JOCKEY #7. ARABIAN #8. PADDOCK
Answer: PALOMINO

72. **Jumbles:** #1. REDS #2. TWINS #3. TIGERS #4. BRAVES #5. YANKEES #6. MARLINS #7. DODGERS #8. CARDINALS
Answer: DIAMONDBACKS

73. **Jumbles:** #1. ALDA #2. KOREA #3. RADAR #4. MAJOR #5. POTTER #6. KLINGER #7. CAPTAIN #8. TRAPPER #9. DOCTORS
Answer: OPERATING ROOM

74. **Jumbles:** #1. FUDGE #2. HONEY #3. DINNER #4. POULTRY #5. POPCORN #6. SEAFOOD #7. FROSTING
Answer: FRESH FRUIT

75. **Jumbles:** #1. CROWS #2. HYENAS #3. ZEBRAS #4. WHALES #5. TURKEYS #6. BADGERS #7. DOLPHINS
Answer: KANGAROOS

76. **Jumbles:** #1. FOG #2. LOOK #3. CLICK #4. TROPHY #5. BALANCE #6. HUMIDITY #7. INFECTION #8. TRANSPLANT #9. PREHISTORIC #10. INTELLECTUAL
Answer: AUTOBIOGRAPHY

77. **Jumbles:** #1. GRIEF—BLISS #2. ROUGH—SMOOTH #3. STUPID—CLEVER #4. SUNKEN—AFLOAT #5. DETAIN—RELEASE
Answer: DARK—LIGHT

78. **Jumbles:** #1. NUTTY #2. VERIFY #3. CHANGE #4. TROPHY #5. GAMBLE #6. WALLOP
Answers: #1. NOVEL #2. AUTHOR #3. HEMINGWAY

79. **Jumbles:** #1. RIGHT #2. THOUGHT #3. CHILDREN #4. BEHAVE #5. GREENER
Answer: COVET

80. **Jumbles:** #1. FIVE + FIVE = TEN #2. EIGHT x ONE = EIGHT #3. TWO − TWO = FOUR − FOUR #4. TWELVE ÷ TWELVE = ONE #5. ONE + ONE = FIVE − THREE
Answer: THREE x THREE = NINE

81. **Jumbles:** #1. BLUEBERRIES #2. HOPSCOTCH #3. ICE SCREAMS #4. GRANDPAW #5. YOUR BREATH #6. CRACK IT UP #7. MILK SHAKES

82. **Jumbles:** #1. EAGLE #2. LLAMA #3. CAMEL #4. MONKEY #5. GIRAFFE #6. MUSKRAT
Answer: LEMMING

83. **Jumbles:** #1. IDAHO #2. ALASKA #3. OREGON #4. VERMONT #5. WYOMING #6. VIRGINIA #7. MISSOURI
Answer: MARYLAND

84. **Jumbles:** #1. PIMPLE #2. INVOKE #3. COLLAR #4. FORAGE #5. DOSAGE #6. MANIAC #7. HELMET
Answers: #1. DRAMA #2. MOVIE #3. MAFIA #4. CASINO

85. **Jumbles:** #1. PATIO #2. SIDING #3. CLOSET #4. WINDOW #5. BATHTUB #6. BALCONY #7. DRIVEWAY
Answer: CARPETING

86. **Jumbles:** #1. CRAB #2. HAWK #3. EAGLE #4. SLOTH #5. BABOON #6. MONKEY #7. AARDVARK
Answer: WALLABY

87. **Jumbles:** #1. OUNCE #2. AVENUE #3. SECOND #4. NUMBER #5. FREEWAY #6. BUILDING #7. DISTANCE
Answer: DECEMBER

88. **Jumbles:** #1. HOPI #2. YUMA #3. GORGE #4. CACTUS #5. NAVAJO #6. INDIANS #7. PHOENIX #8. FLAGSTAFF
Answer: GRAND CANYON

89. **Jumbles:** #1. FOLD #2. WILD #3. FLUSH #4. BLUFF #5. BETTING #6. STRAIGHT
Answer: FULL HOUSE

90. **Jumbles:** #1. EGYPT #2. RUSSIA #3. TURKEY #4. JORDAN #5. LIBERIA #6. BELGIUM
Answer: PORTUGAL

91. **Jumbles:** #1. FELL—SPELL #2. MOSS—GLOSS #3. BUMPY—GRUMPY #4. STENCH—TRENCH #5. LIZARD—WIZARD
Answer: NUDGE—FUDGE

92. **Jumbles:** #1. KITTEN #2. SUITOR #3. DISMAL #4. HAZARD #5. UPROOT #6. CAMPER
Answers: #1. PANAMA #2. ISTHMUS

93. **Jumbles:** #1. FRANK #2. PUDDY #3. COSMO #4. ELAINE #5. GEORGE #6. NEWMAN #7. MAILMAN #8. NEIGHBOR
Answer: COMEDIAN

94. **Jumbles:** #1. WINDY #2. ICICLE #3. CHILLY #4. CLIMATE #5. DEGREES #6. DROUGHT #7. BLIZZARD
Answer: TWISTER

95. **Jumbles:** #1. HAIL #2. BLUNT #3. CROSS #4. SINGLE #5. MATTER #6. GROUND #7. KNUCKLE
Answer: GRUMBLE

96. **Jumbles:** #1. A BIG STINK #2. SPOILED MILK #3. A WEBSITE #4. A FAUCET #5. YOUR PICTURE #6. I AM STUFFED #7. A SWALLOW

97. **Jumbles:** #1. BESS #2. BETTY #3. DOLLEY #4. HANNAH #5. MARTHA #6. HILLARY #7. BARBARA #8. ELEANOR
Answer: ROSALYNN

98. **Jumbles:** #1. INEPT #2. CRAZY #3. FINITE #4. INTACT #5. EXOTIC #6. LETHAL #7. VULGAR #8. DISTANT
Answer: CONVENIENT

99. **Jumbles:** #1. HAVANA, CUBA #2. TOKYO, JAPAN #3. PARIS, FRANCE #4. ATHENS, GREECE 5. MOSCOW, RUSSIA #6. LONDON, ENGLAND
Answer: DUBLIN, IRELAND

100. **Jumbles:** #1. BULLET #2. TREATY #3. TARGET #4. AIRCRAFT #5. INFANTRY #6. BLOCKADE
Answer: BATTLEFIELD

101. **Jumbles:** #1. OUTFIT #2. TUXEDO #3. SHORTS #4. GLOVES #5. UNIFORM #6. GARMENT #7. SWEATER
Answer: NIGHTGOWN

102. **Jumbles:** #1. CHILE #2. TURKEY #3. JORDAN #4. POLAND #5. LIBERIA #6. HUNGARY #7. ROMANIA
Answer: PORTUGAL

103. **Jumbles:** #1. FILM #2. CHAIR #3. PROPS #4. SCRIPT #5. RETAKE #6. MAKEUP #7. EFFECTS
Answer: REHEARSAL

104. **Jumbles:** #1. PAPER #2. PENCIL #3. SKETCH #4. CANVAS #5. ERASER #6. CRAYON
Answer: ART CLASS

105. **Jumbles:** #1. BOISE #2. TOPEKA #3. LINCOLN #4. PHOENIX #5. OLYMPIA #6. TRENTON #7. RICHMOND
Answer: INDIANAPOLIS

106. **Jumbles:** #1. LIGHT #2. LUNGE #3. LAVISH #4. LETTER #5. LENGTH #6. LAGOON #7. LANDING #8. LEISURE
Answer: LAUGHTER

107. **Jumbles:** #1. ROOKIE #2. FUMBLE #3. SOFTBALL #4. SCHEDULE #5. SWIMMING #6. STANDING
Answer: TOUCHDOWN

108. **Jumbles:** #1. ACE #2. BOOK #3. RADIO #4. MANAGE #5. BALLOON #6. ACCIDENT #7. INFLATION #8. UNDERSTOOD #9. IMPROVEMENT #10. UNREASONABLE
Answer: UNCONDITIONAL

109. **Jumbles:** #1. ALLEY #2. COACH #3. WOODY #4. DANSON #5. BOSTON #6. FRASIER #7. PITCHER #8. SHELLEY #9. WAITRESS
Answer: BARTENDER

110. **Jumbles:** #1. ECHO #2. IDAHO #3. OMEGA #4. ADVICE #5. ABLAZE #6. ESKIMO #7. AUSTRIA
Answer: AVOCADO

111. **Jumbles:** #1. ROCKY #2. CONTACT #3. FANTASIA #4. HOOSIERS #5. CHINATOWN #6. THE INSIDER #7. TAXI DRIVER
Answer: THE EXORCIST

112. Jumbles: #1. FIVE PLUS FIVE = TEN
#2. ONE MINUS ONE = ZERO
#3. SIX PLUS THREE = NINE
#4. SEVEN MINUS FIVE = TWO
#5. TWO TIMES FOUR = EIGHT
Answer: SIX PLUS FIVE = ELEVEN

113. Jumbles: #1. LIGHT #2. FLASH
#3. FOCUS #4. COLOR #5. BLURRY
#6. CONTRAST #7. EXPOSURE
Answer: SHUTTER

114. Jumbles: #1. OHIO #2. MORGAN #3. PATENTS
#4. INVENTOR #5. DEAFNESS
#6. NEW JERSEY #7. LABORATORY
Answer: THOMAS EDISON

115. Jumbles: #1. SIX + FIVE = ELEVEN
#2. EIGHTY ÷ FOUR = TWENTY
#3. TEN + TEN = TWENTY + ZERO
#4. THIRTY + THIRTY = SIXTY
#5. TWO x FOUR = TWELVE – FOUR
Answer: EIGHT x TWO = SIXTEEN

116. Jumbles: #1. HARSH—BRASH
#2. ENJOY—RELISH #3. BRAVE—FEARLESS
#4. GATHER—COLLECT
#5. SHRINK—DWINDLE
Answer: WRECK—DESTROY

117. Jumbles: #1. FLOOD #2. SICKLE #3. BUCKLE
#4. COHORT #5. COCOON #6. STATION
Answers: #1. FOOD #2. COOKBOOK
#3. INSTRUCTIONS

118. Jumbles: #1. BANKER #2. AUTHOR
#3. WAITER #4. CASHIER #5. SURGEON
#6. MUSICIAN
Answer: MECHANIC

119. Jumbles: #1. SPRAIN #2. DOCTOR
#3. WEIGHT #4. ASPIRIN #5. FATIGUE
#6. HOSPITAL #7. FRACTURE
Answer: HEADACHE

120. Jumbles: #1. CRUSH #2. SPIRAL #3. VANISH
#4. SAVAGE #5. BEYOND #6. MANAGE
#7. DRIZZLE
Answers: #1. CUBA #2. ISLAND #3. HAVANA
#4. SPANISH

121. Jumbles: #1. OPERA #2. VIOLIN #3. MOZART
#4. ALLEGRO #5. CONCERT #6. MEASURE
#7. HARMONY
Answer: OVERTURE

122. Jumbles: #1. NOUN #2. NOVEL #3. NUDGE
#4. NATIVE #5. NEEDLE #6. NIMBLE
#7. NARROW #8. NOTHING
Answer: NEIGHBOR

123. Jumbles: #1. BRIDGE #2. TRACKS
#3. BOXCAR #4. EXPRESS #5. WHISTLE
#6. CABOOSE #7. ENGINEER
Answer: PASSENGER

124. Jumbles: #1. JOHN TYLER #2. JAMES POLK
#3. JOHN ADAMS #4. GERALD FORD
#5. HERBERT HOOVER #6. CHESTER ARTHUR
#7. ANDREW JACKSON
Answer: JAMES MONROE

125. Jumbles: #1. ROSS #2. RICHIE #3. FONZIE
#4. JOANIE #5. COUSIN #6. MOTHER
#7. HOWARD #8. MARRIAGE #9. HARDWARE
Answer: THE CUNNINGHAMS

126. Jumbles: #1. BISON #2. PANDA #3. LEMUR
#4. RACCOON #5. ELEPHANT #6. MANDRILL
#7. CHIPMUNK
Answer: ARMADILLO

127. Jumbles: #1. VALUE #2. BANKER #3. SALARY
#4. INCOME #5. WALLET #6. REVENUE
#7. INTEREST #8. BILLFOLD
Answer: ONE DOLLAR BILL

128. Jumbles: #1. DANDY #2. JUROR #3. COPIER
#4. TAVERN #5. GUSHER #6. MASCOT
Answers: #1. JUPITER #2. ROMAN GOD

129. Jumbles: #1. ROOK #2. PAWN #3. MOVE
#4. PIECE #5. KNIGHT #6. BISHOP
#7. CAPTURE #8. DEFENSE
Answer: CHECKMATE

130. Jumbles: #1. SIGHT #2. SHOULD #3. MERGE
#4. RUNNING #5. PONDER #6. CERTAIN
Answer: CONGESTION

131. Jumbles: #1. YOGI #2. BIKINI #3. SAFARI
#4. SALAMI #5. RAVIOLI #6. HIBACHI
#7. ZUCCHINI
Answer: BROCCOLI

132. Jumbles: #1. GRAVE #2. PERCH #3. POWER
#4. BOTTOM #5. DISTURB #6. FORMULA
Answers: #1. PROGRAM #2. SOFTWARE
#3. COMPUTER

133. Jumbles: #1. DATA #2. CLICK #3. MOUSE
#4. DELETE #5. MEMORY #6. PENTIUM
#7. PROGRAM #8. KEYBOARD
Answer: BILL GATES

134. Jumbles: #1. POP #2. WALK #3. CLAMP
#4. ESCAPE #5. MONITOR #6. WHITECAP
#7. MATERNITY #8. FACILITATE
#9. APPROXIMATE #10. MISADVENTURE
Answer: EXTRAORDINARY

135. Jumbles: #1. DECAY #2. CROWN #3. BRACES
#4. PLAQUE #5. ENAMEL #6. FILLING
Answer: FLUORIDE

136. Jumbles: #1. ARUBA #2. MALTA #3. HAWAII
#4. TAIWAN #5. MIDWAY #6. ICELAND
#7. BERMUDA #8. GREENLAND
Answer: MANHATTAN

137. Jumbles: #1. PINKEYE #2. REDWOOD
#3. GREENERY #4. WHITECAPS
#5. BLACKJACK #6. GREYHOUND
Answer: GREENLAND

138. Jumbles: #1. TEN – TEN = ZERO
#2. FIVE ÷ FIVE = ONE
#3. FOUR x FIVE = TWENTY
#4. SIX + SIX = FIVE + SEVEN
#5. ELEVEN + TWO = THIRTEEN
Answer: TWELVE ÷ FOUR = THREE

139. Jumbles: #1. STRICT #2. TWITCH #3. MYSTIC
#4. REFUND #5. STEAMY #6. BESTOW
#7. LONGEST
Answers: #1. WIND #2. STORMY
#3. CYCLONE #4. TWISTER

140. Jumbles: #1. MULES #2. RABBITS
#3. BEAVERS #4. BUFFALO #5. CHICKENS
#6. GIRAFFES #7. GORILLAS
Answer: FLAMINGOS

141. Jumbles: #1. PULPIT #2. TATTLE #3. DINNER
#4. REFLEX #5. IGUANA #6. BOUNCE
Answer: #1. BUILDING #2. STRUCTURE

142. Jumbles: #1. IODINE #2. COBALT #3. HELIUM
#4. OXYGEN #5. SODIUM #6. CALCIUM
#7. URANIUM
Answer: ALUMINUM

143. Jumbles: #1. FLASK #2. BANDIT #3. DISCUS
#4. TYRANT #5. GLANCE #6. NORMAL
Answers: #1. AFRICA #2. LANDMASS
#3. CONTINENT

144. Jumbles: #1. NIGERIA #2. AUSTRIA
#3. URUGUAY #4. GERMANY #5. MOROCCO
#6. ETHIOPIA #7. THAILAND
Answer: MADAGASCAR

145. Jumbles: #1. GABBY #2. AWAKE #3. FEISTY
#4. GUILTY #5. HORRID #6. CUDDLY
#7. CUSTOM #8. GLOOMY
Answer: COMFORTABLE

146. Jumbles: #1. BARREN #2. STATION #3. PLATEAU #4. PENGUIN #5. COLDEST #6. SOUTHERN
Answer: GLACIERS

147. Jumbles: #1. ROCKY #2. GANDHI #3. TITANIC #4. PLATOON #5. RAIN MAN #6. THE STING #7. GLADIATOR #8. UNFORGIVEN
Answer: THE GODFATHER

148. Jumbles: #1. VACUUM #2. COSMOS #3. GRAVITY #4. JUPITER #5. ECLIPSE #6. SUNSPOT
Answer: UNIVERSE

149. Jumbles: #1. KOALA #2. MOUSE #3. JACKAL #4. BOBCAT #5. OCELOT #6. OSTRICH #7. TORTOISE
Answer: CARIBOU

150. Jumbles: #1. MUSHY #2. PICKLE #3. GENDER #4. OBJECT #5. ENOUGH #6. FALSIFY
Answers: #1. PENGUIN #2. FLIGHTLESS

151. Jumbles: #1. SICK #2. SEIZE #3. SWEET #4. SCENIC #5. SALARY #6. SCARCE #7. SHADOW #8. SHERIFF
Answer: SANDWICH

152. Jumbles: #1. BIT #2. PUNT #3. FINAL #4. SECOND #5. SOLVENT #6. EXPLICIT #7. INFLUENCE #8. MEMORANDUM #9. GINGERBREAD #10. CONSTITUTION
Answer: PRONUNCIATION

153. Jumbles: #1. HOMER #2. INNING #3. LEAGUE #4. SEASON #5. DRIBBLE #6. CRICKET #7. VICTORY #8. CAPTAIN
Answer: SIDELINE

154. Jumbles: #1. BEACH #2. GRASS #3. TUNDRA #4. CANYON #5. GROUND #6. CLIMATE #7. PLATEAU
Answer: LONGITUDE

155. Jumbles: #1. AFRICA #2. JUNGLE #3. PHOTOS #4. ENGLAND #5. TANZANIA #6. CAMBRIDGE
Answer: JANE GOODALL

156. Jumbles: #1. GHOST #2. DUMBO #3. CASINO #4. PAYBACK #5. RAIN MAN #6. MAGNOLIA #7. GLADIATOR
Answer: GROUNDHOG DAY

157. Jumbles: #1. CHEST #2. FIBULA #3. SPLEEN #4. THROAT #5. TONGUE #6. TRACHEA #7. FOREARM
Answer: CARTILAGE

158. Jumbles: #1. EIGHT ÷ FOUR = TWO #2. FIVE x FOUR = TWENTY #3. SIX + SIX = ONE DOZEN #4. SIX + SEVEN = THIRTEEN #5. ONE HUNDRED ÷ TEN = TEN
Answer: ONE + FIVE = THREE + THREE

159. Jumbles: #1. LOSS—PROFIT #2. FINAL—INITIAL #3. VACANT—OCCUPIED #4. VALLEY—MOUNTAIN #5. SOLVENT—BANKRUPT
Answer: FACT—FICTION

160. Jumbles: #1. RAVEN #2. OSPREY #3. MAGPIE #4. VULTURE #5. MALLARD #6. BLUEBIRD #7. CARDINAL #8. COCKATOO
Answer: BALD EAGLE

161. Jumbles: #1. TRENCH #2. JUMBLE #3. LOATHE #4. COHORT #5. OTTAWA #6. FUNERAL
Answers: #1. ATHLETE #2. FOOTBALL #3. JOE NAMATH

162. Jumbles: #1. CANNON #2. OFFICER #3. ADMIRAL #4. SAMURAI #5. FLOTILLA #6. PRISONER #7. PENTAGON
Answer: AIRCRAFT CARRIER

163. Jumbles: #1. DEMI MOORE #2. RENE RUSSO #3. BING CROSBY #4. MARK HAMILL #5. KEVIN KLINE #6. GLENN CLOSE
Answer: MEL GIBSON

164. Jumbles: #1. FABRIC #2. NEEDLE #3. BUTTON #4. THIMBLE #5. MACHINE #6. SCISSORS
Answer: ALTERATION

165. Jumbles: #1. SWIFT #2. SHIFTY #3. WICKED #4. SADDLE #5. LAWYER #6. ONTARIO #7. AMNESIA
Answers: #1. WESTERN #2. RAWHIDE #3. EASTWOOD

166. Jumbles: #1. FLAKE #2. FLOOD #3. DEGREE #4. RAINBOW #5. MONSOON #6. RAINFALL #7. HUMIDITY #8. DOWNPOUR
Answer: LOW PRESSURE

167. Jumbles: #1. HARRY TRUMAN #2. JAMES MONROE #3. RICHARD NIXON #4. JAMES MADISON #5. LYNDON JOHNSON #6. WARREN HARDING
Answer: ANDREW JOHNSON

168. Jumbles: #1. TRICK #2. PADDLE #3. MORSEL #4. ARIZONA #5. MYSTERY #6. WHIMPER #7. WELCOME
Answers: #1. WATER #2. OLYMPIC #3. SWIMMER #4. MARK SPITZ

169. Jumbles: #1. SPLICE #2. DISPEL #3. BUNDLE #4. COUPON #5. MUSCLE #6. AMERICA #7. NEGATIVE
Answers: #1. ENCORE #2. AUDIENCE #3. APPLAUSE

170. Jumbles: #1. TWO TIMES TWO = FOUR #2. TEN PLUS TEN = TWENTY #3. FIVE PLUS SIX = ELEVEN #4. EIGHT MINUS EIGHT = ZERO #5. NINE PLUS SEVEN = SIXTEEN
Answer: SEVEN MINUS TWO = FIVE

171. Jumbles: #1. MAN #2. PILL #3. VOGUE #4. FIERCE #5. PROGRAM #6. BLACKOUT #7. INTERSECT #8. MATCHMAKER #9. PUNCTUATION #10. MOUNTAINSIDE
Answer: CONFIGURATION

172. Jumbles: #1. HARVARD #2. NINETEEN #3. SOFTWARE #4. MICROSOFT #5. WEALTHIEST #6. WASHINGTON #7. BILLIONAIRE
Answer: BILL GATES

173. Jumbles: #1. FELINE #2. CANINE #3. SCURRY #4. FORAGE #5. VERMIN #6. MAMMAL #7. CRITTER #8. SPECIES
Answer: CREATURE

174. Jumbles: #1. TAXI #2. ALICE #3. HOTEL #4. COSBY #5. DALLAS #6. HUNTER #7. CHEERS #8. FLIPPER #9. COLUMBO
Answer: ALL IN THE FAMILY

175. Jumbles: #1. NAVY #2. BOMB #3. BULLET #4. ATTACK #5. ROCKET #6. HELMET #7. GUNFIRE #8. CHOPPER #9. ADMIRAL
Answer: CAMOUFLAGE

176. Jumbles: #1. BOISE #2. AUSTIN #3. PIERRE #4. HELENA #5. BOSTON #6. RALEIGH #7. JACKSON #8. TRENTON #9. COLUMBUS
Answer: HARRISBURG

177. Jumbles: #1. HARP #2. PIANO #3. GUITAR #4. MELODY #5. PICCOLO #6. CONCERT #7. BASSOON #8. MEASURE #9. MANDOLIN
Answer: HARMONICA

178. Jumbles: #1. SKUNK #2. GOOSE #3. PIGEON #4. FERRET #5. JACKAL #6. WEASEL #7. WALRUS #8. PENGUIN #9. PANTHER
Answer: PORCUPINE

Do You Know Any Kids?

If you'd like to see kids use their

`RAISBN`

to develop skills that could help them get ahead in

`CSOLOH`

then you should

`NOSICERD`

buying them *Jumble® BrainBusters Junior*. It's packed full of fun puzzles covering a wide range of subjects.

JUMBLE BrainBusters! Junior

U.S. STATE CAPITALS

Unscramble the Jumbles, one letter to each square, to spell U.S. state capitals.

#1 `EEHANL`

#2 `EUAJUN`

#3 `TATNAAL`

#4 `RENTONT`

#5 `PLYIAMO`

Arrange the circled letters to solve the mystery answer.

MYSTERY ANSWER

Montgomery · Juneau · Phoenix · Little Rock · Sacramento · Denver · Hartford · Dover · Tallahassee · Atlanta · Honolulu · Boise · Springfield · Indianapolis · Des Moines · Topeka · Frankfort

Baton Rouge · Augusta · Annapolis · Boston · Lansing · St. Paul · Jackson · Jefferson City · Helena · Lincoln · Carson City · Concord · Trenton · Santa Fe · Albany · Raleigh · Bismarck

Columbus · Oklahoma City · Salem · Harrisburg · Providence · Columbia · Pierre · Nashville · Austin · Salt Lake City · Montpelier · Richmond · Olympia · Charleston · Madison · Cheyenne

Box of Clues

Stumped? Maybe you can find a clue below.

-Georgia   -Hawaii
-Alaska   -Washington
-New Jersey -Montana

Need More Jumbles®?

Jumble® Books

Animal Jumble®
$9.95 • ISBN 1-57243-197-0

Jumble® at Work
$9.95 • ISBN 1-57243-147-4

Jumble® Fun
$9.95 • ISBN 1-57243-379-5

Jumble® Grab Bag
$9.95 • ISBN 1-57243-273-X

Jumble® Jubilee
$9.95 • ISBN 1-57243-231-4

Jumble® Junction
$9.95 • ISBN 1-57243-380-9

Jumble® Madness
$9.95 • ISBN 1-892049-24-4

Jumble® See & Search
$9.95 • ISBN 1-57243-549-6

Jumble® Surprise
$9.95 • ISBN 1-57243-320-5

Romance Jumble®
$9.95 • ISBN 1-57243-146-6

Sports Jumble®
$9.95 • ISBN 1-57243-113-X

Summer Fun Jumble®
$9.95 • ISBN 1-57243-114-8

Travel Jumble®
$9.95 • ISBN 1-57243-198-9

TV Jumble®
$9.95 • ISBN 1-57243-462-7

Oversize Jumble® Books

Generous Jumble®
$19.95 • ISBN 1-57243-385-X

Giant Jumble®
$19.95 • ISBN 1-57243-349-3

Gigantic Jumble®
$19.95 • ISBN 1-57243-426-0

Jumbo Jumble®
$19.95 • ISBN 1-57243-314-0

Colossal Jumble®
$19.95 • ISBN 1-57243-490-2

More than 500 puzzles each!

Jumble® Crosswords™

More than 175 puzzles each!

Jumble® Crosswords™
$9.95 • ISBN 1-57243-347-7

More Jumble® Crosswords™
$9.95 • ISBN 1-57243-386-8

Jumble® Crosswords™ Adventure
$9.95 • ISBN 1-57243-462-7

Jumble® Crosswords™ Challenge
$9.95 • ISBN 1-57243-423-6

Jumble® BrainBusters

Jumble® BrainBusters
$9.95 • ISBN: 1-892049-28-7

Jumble® BrainBusters II
$9.95 • ISBN: 1-57243-424-4

Jumble® BrainBusters III
$9.95 • ISBN: 1-57243-463-5

Jumble® BrainBusters IV
$9.95 • ISBN: 1-57243-489-9

More than 175 puzzles each!

Jumble® BrainBusters Junior

More than 175 puzzles each!

Jumble® BrainBusters Junior
$9.95 • ISBN: 1-892049-29-5

Jumble® BrainBusters Junior II
$9.95 • ISBN: 1-57243-425-2